STUMBLING

Life's Great Lessons in Overcoming Challenges, Trials and Pains

MARISSA L. MAGCAWAS

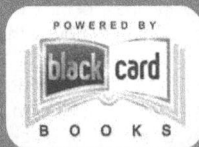

POWERED BY

black card

BOOKS

Author: Marissa L. Magcawas

Title: Stumbling

ISBN: 978-1-77204-243-6

Category: SELF-HELP/Motivational & Inspirational

Publisher: Black Card Books

Division of Gerry Robert Enterprises Inc.

Suite 214, 5-18 Ringwood Drive

Stouffville, Ontario, Canada, L4A 0N2

International Calling: +1 877 280 8736

www.blackcardbooks.com

. . . .

Printed in Canada

TABLE OF CONTENTS

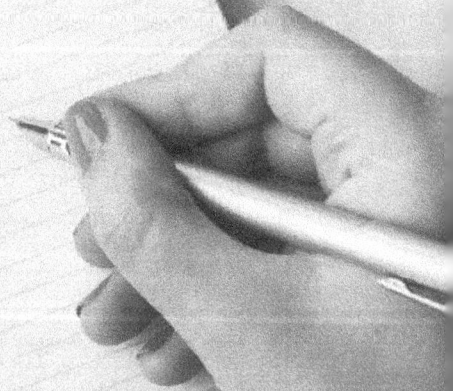

ACKNOWLEDGMENTS

Having an idea and turning it into a book is harder than I thought it would be. It took me a long time to finish it — about six years from its conception to its completion. Truthfully, I never thought I would be able to finalize the book, considering my mental health condition, but I never gave up. The experience was very challenging, yet highly rewarding. Life's all about the journey, and I've learned so much about myself during this process. At the same time, there are so many people to thank who helped make this dream become a reality. I'm forever grateful and indebted.

I want to thank God most of all, because without Him I wouldn't be able to do this. He provided the courage, strength, guidance and wisdom. Thank you, God!

I especially want to thank the individuals who provided the support, encouragement and expertise to make this book happen. Sincerest thanks to my publisher, Gerry Robert, who showed me how this was possible by personally mentoring me. I have felt honored to have your support.

Annie Ramos, my Project Coordinator — thank you for being very understanding and encouraging during this process and for having faith in my abilities; you have been amazing.

My editor, Gail Westerfield, thank you for your valuable advice and recommendations; I've enjoyed working with you.

To Louie Vail Acosta, the VP for Production & Administration — I am grateful for your support. I sincerely appreciate the significant information and advice you have shared with me.

ACKNOWLEDGMENTS

To Chris Dyson, my heartfelt thanks for your patience, support and understanding and for giving me the extension to finish this book.

To those I have designated "The Power of 26," namely, Bernard Dalziel, Billy Tugano, Dr. Neneng Galanto, Evelyn Miranda, Gem Thater, Gertie Leano, Gina Pinangat, Janeth Anguluan, John Edwards, Joji Lassam, Joven Magcawas, Julieta Dioquino, Leila Magcawas, Lina Dichoso, Maidee Mabale, Maria Greaves, Maria V, Nancy Martinez, Ning Mah, Nori Lumbera-Villaruel, Norman Carriere, Perla Martinez, Remilia Lopez Chiong, Rohan Baichu, Vernon Magcawas and Yolanda Tanciangco: I feel so fortunate to have been able to connect with such awe-inspiring people whose real-life stories have encouraged many. You willingly gave your time to make a valuable contribution to the content of this book. Thank you for your trust in sharing your inspiring and amazing life stories. I want to let you know how much I appreciate you; this means a lot to me.

From reading early drafts to giving me advice on the cover and giving me motivation and encouragement, I'm forever grateful to my very good friend, Anthony Carrol. You stood by me during every struggle I encountered in this book journey. Thank you for your patience, trust and faith in me that I could do this. You believe in me even when I don't believe in myself. For that, I am eternally grateful.

I am truly lucky to count on the support and encouragement of my precious friends, especially Don Wolfe, for his honest opinion on the book cover.

Finally, I would like to express my deep and sincere gratitude to my wonderful family – my superb brothers and sisters – for their continuous and unparalleled love, help and support. I am also forever indebted to my parents, Ernita and Osias Magcawas, for their unconditional love. It was their love that raised me up. They helped me in every step of my life; they trained us all very well for life's challenges and have made me who I am. Now that this book is written, I would just love to see how joyous and proud my parents would be if they were still alive.

To my son, Tyrell: I want you to know that I value and respect your opinion. I really appreciate your help, love, encouragement, endless patience and belief in me. Your kind words in your beautiful message warmed my heart. Thank you from the bottom of my heart.

I want to thank *everyone* – if I missed your names – who in one way or another has said something positive to me or has taught me something that has contributed to the completion of this book. I heard it all and nothing is taken for granted; it meant something. I appreciate you.

FOREWORD

When I first met Marissa in one of the writer's workshop; I remembered her approaching me and thanking me – with so much joy and excitement, finally *"my dream of writing a book will be achieved!"* She told me briefly that she's undergoing chemotherapy and had actually taken off her head scarf to show me her bald hair. She said she's so thrilled to write her beautiful breast cancer journey and her amazing life story. I am so impressed! I knew her book will be remarkable.

Marissa Magcawas is a single mother and a breast cancer survivor. She had experienced wrongful dismissal and was diagnosed with depression and post-traumatic stress disorder (PTSD) when she had a car accident. She had been through good times and bad times but has always stayed optimistic and strong. Time and again, she has stumbled but got up and keep moving forward. She made choices from a place of power and not from a place of brokenness. What an inspiration! I'm proud of all that she's lived through.

Marissa is the best person to write this book entitled *Stumbling: Life's Great Lessons In Overcoming Challenges, Trials and Pains* that depicts her trials, challenges, trauma and heartbreak; and it definitely is her own story to tell and share.

In her book, The Power of 26 is a powerful concept whose true life stories of amazing individuals have inspired many people. They talked about their stumbles, their struggles and wins – we can learn life's great lessons.

The simple, practical ways in overcoming challenges, trials and pains presented in this book are proven and tested to have worked wonders and can benefit anyone as they go through life.

This book can enrich anyone who reads it... very touching and inspirational book. May this book be a beacon of light for those who are single parents, who are giving up, undergoing breast cancer, depression and feeling hopeless.

—Gerry Robert

Speaker and international bestselling author of *The Millionaire Mindset*, *Multiply Your Business* and *Publish a Book & Grow Rich*

www.gerryrobert.com

INTRODUCTION

Amidst the everyday challenges of being a single mother while battling breast cancer, experiencing wrongful dismissal and overcoming depression and post-traumatic stress disorder (PTSD), how do I deal with my life on a daily basis? It has been very tough; at times, I just wanted to end it all...

Indeed, all of us go through life's struggles, challenges, trials and pains. But it's not how we stumble or fall that matters most but how we get up. As Ben Okri says, "The most authentic thing about us is our capacity to create, to overcome, to endure, to transform, to love and to be greater than our suffering." This is the very reason why I have finally decided to write this book.

I've been through a lot, just like any other human being. It is not easy to really share these adversities in my life, particularly my depression, due to the stigma against mental health disorders that still exists. This is my most vulnerable moment, and I'm proud of myself. There's something that happens when you have an illness: It makes you look at the world in a different way. I experienced a change in my perspective that focuses more on the important things in my life – those things that add meaning and higher purpose.

I want to share the moments that contributed to the person I am today. This book entitled *Stumbling: Life's Great Lessons In Overcoming Challenges, Trials and Pains* depicts my trials, challenges, trauma and heartbreak, and it definitely is my own story to tell and share. I discuss how I overcame my challenges as a single mother, my beautiful breast cancer journey and my ongoing battle with depression. More importantly, I share the lessons I have learned from overcoming these struggles, trials and pains. Simple ways you can cope with your challenges, weather the storm and bounce back beautifully – shifting your mind creatively and emerging as a winner in your own unique way – are also presented here.

In this book, you will find "The Power of 26," which I also call "The A to Zen of Life." According to *www.sunsigns.org/angel-number-26-meaning*, number 26 depicts happiness, sorrows, joys and hardships but also encourages us to maintain a positive outlook on things. And just like how life is portrayed in this book by 26 amazing individuals. They are remarkable friends, colleagues, brothers and sisters whom I interviewed. They are extraordinary people who shared their inspirational stories, nuggets of wisdom, the hardest struggles they had experienced and how they conquered them.

For all of the readers who are affected by some health concerns, I understand and share your feelings of pain and frustration. I know how hard it is, but remember that you are not alone, and there is a greater purpose for all of your suffering. Have faith in God and believe in the power of prayer. We grow by experiencing hardships and tribulations; to those of us who believe in God, undergoing hardships and breakthroughs is God's greatest blessings.

Have the right mindset, as well. This is crucial to succeeding in life and also reduces the risk of mental and physical illnesses. Furthermore, develop an attitude of gratitude; practice random act of kindness. These are some ways to overcome challenges which in turn became life's great lessons that I have implemented in my journey, these strategies have been proven and I'm an example. I applied these techniques and they worked successfully and continuously. I sincerely hope that these ways work for you, too, and that they help you to feel good about yourself.

If I can inspire one person or two, make someone smile, and make a difference through this book, it is truly a remarkable gift. May this book be a beacon of light for those who are giving up and feeling hopeless.

Life is a journey filled with lessons, hardships, heartaches, joys, celebrations and special moments that we need to embrace and appreciate fully. The road will not always be smooth; in fact, throughout our travels, we will encounter many challenges and adversities. However, when we're faced with a challenge, we learn more about ourselves – what we're made of, what we can handle, how we react to something distressing and how strong we are. Remember that adversity builds champions.

It's been said that in life, if you ever stumble, make it a part of your dance. Learn from your mistakes and keep trying. Just realize your potential and shine with your strengths. Take time to celebrate both your successes and failures. Choose to maintain a positive attitude. Be happy. Find the humor and the goodness in everything, and you will feel good. Feeling good brings rewards of joy, love and peace. Be loving and generous. Surround yourself with positive people and energy. Look forward to each new day with the excitement and wonder of a small child; we can always push our "child buttons" when we need them the most. It's actually fun! Live slowly, simplify living and savor your life.

My journey of writing this book is incredible, a story of its own – with a great many lessons learned, combined with problems that came up during the writing. With my depression and PTSD, writing can be tough and stressful, especially when my brain doesn't cooperate. It is so hard to have the motivation to write and the focus, considering there's a deadline. It was torture at times. Actually, I never thought I would be able to finish the book, but I did not give up. I'm really thankful and grateful that I persevered.

While writing this book, I've learned that life is tough, but I need to be tougher. Before I write, I say my prayers, and I lift it all to God, so that He will take control of my whole being and my thoughts. I have learned to listen to my heart because it always tells me what to do and is usually right; I trust the process all the way. It has taught me to be present, to be calm and to be grateful for whatever I have – especially the simplest, precious little things.

This is my life; it is the true game, not a rehearsal. There are no second chances, and I only get one shot at it. I must not take it for granted, and I'm solely responsible and accountable for it. We have to attack any moment in our lives like it's the last chance we get.

During my life's journey, there have been good times and bad times, but to the core, I have stayed optimistic. I've had my share of breakups, breakdowns and breakthroughs. I have stumbled; I have gotten up. I made choices from a place of power, not from a place of brokenness. I'm proud of all that I've lived through. I have made it this far in life, and that in itself is a huge accomplishment. I have a very successful business-owner friend; he always tells me that I inspire him so much – that every time I stumble, I get back up and just keep moving forward. So, wherever your life takes you, trust your journey and give it a chance: I did. I believe that if I can make it through everything that I did, then I can make it through anything.

Lastly, I would like to share a quote taken from Rishika Jain Inspirations: "In the race of life, don't waste your energy and time trying to compare with others. Sometimes you are ahead... Sometimes behind... The race is long, and in the end it's only with yourself." When I'm running against myself, the only thing that matters is that I learn and become better. And it genuinely feels good when I win my races. The hardest races are the best ones. The wins and lessons learned are worth everything.

CHAPTER 1

ON BEING A SINGLE MOM: I BELIEVED I COULD, AND I DID

Every little girl dreams of marrying her own version of Prince Charming, and I was no exception. Although that dream hasn't become a reality yet, I am beyond happy and blessed as a single mother.

"The moment I found out I was pregnant with you, Tyrell, was one of the happiest moments of my life. My giving birth to you was a bit tough, as I labored for about 18 hours, but when I heard your first cry, I cried, too – with joy – and all the pain I had suffered suddenly vanished. This was the most joyful moment of my life. And when I held you in my arms and put you on my chest, skin-to-skin, it was a magical experience; I was elated. You were my precious joy! You have taught me so much about love, kindness,

patience and persistence. You have been a powerful teacher in my life, and I feel so blessed that you chose me to be your mom.

"Tyrell, I know it's hard growing up without a father, and I feel your pain and your anger at times, but I admire you for the kind of person that you are; when I explained the truth, you were there to listen and to do your best to understand, even at a young age. As your mom, the best thing I can do is to hug you so tightly and wish things were different. Know that I love you immensely and that I support all of your dreams and goals – all the way. I know in the core of my being that I've done the best I could in raising you, and I apologize if there have been times when I failed as a mother. Things will never be perfect and will go wrong sometimes. All I ask is that you speak the truth all the days of your life, have God in your life, stay true to yourself and be grateful for what you have. Get an education; it's knowledge that no one can take away from you. Know your worth, and don't let anyone else define it for you. Don't give up; stay strong. If all else fails, have a good cry; it doesn't make you less of a man. Listen to your heart and follow your dreams, specifically your love for football."

Being a single mom is the hardest but the most empowering thing I've ever done. Child-rearing can be difficult under any circumstances and the more so without a partner; it's twice the work and twice the stress, especially juggling work and childcare. It still can be financially difficult, and I have guilt about not spending more time with my son. It's tough to live paycheck to paycheck, having just enough to cover monthly expenses with no money left over and none for savings. I've been in survival mode at times, but I make sure I always have food and all of the basic necessities and that, monthly payments are made.

And fortunately, the father of my son is always there to support us. He may not always be there physically, but he has genuine love, care and concern for his son. We remain good friends. He is a very kind person and a great father to my son. I am thankful for the relationship and the bonding that we have created.

Romantic relationships have not been a strong aspect of my life, particularly because I have my son; it has been my choice to remain single. I prioritize my son and focus in raising him; it can be hard because I have less time to spare for dating, and the fear of getting into a relationship always kicks in. I remember a very good friend who told me that I inspire him a lot for standing tall and never being afraid to be the best mommy and daddy that I could be. He consistently reminds me to celebrate my greatness.

Yes, there are challenges for a single parent, but there are also some exceptional rewards. To mention a few, it has made me feel that I am enough, that I have all the skills and love to raise a child well, and that I can make sound and safe decisions as far as my son's well-being is concerned. Being a single mother is the best part of who I am. It has given me a whole new view of the meaning of life and taught me the true meaning of the words "unconditional love." It truly is the best thing that has ever happened to me.

According to Debolina Raja and Kimberly A. Ludwigsen, "While it is true that parenting is one of the most rewarding jobs in the world, it can also be one of the toughest responsibilities ever, especially If you are a single parent." However, I am grateful to have my family, my friends and my church family, who stood by me and who remain there. As they say, in times of need, you realize who your true support is, and I'm forever grateful for all of the supportive people who helped my son and I thrive: You all make my single parenthood an easy journey.

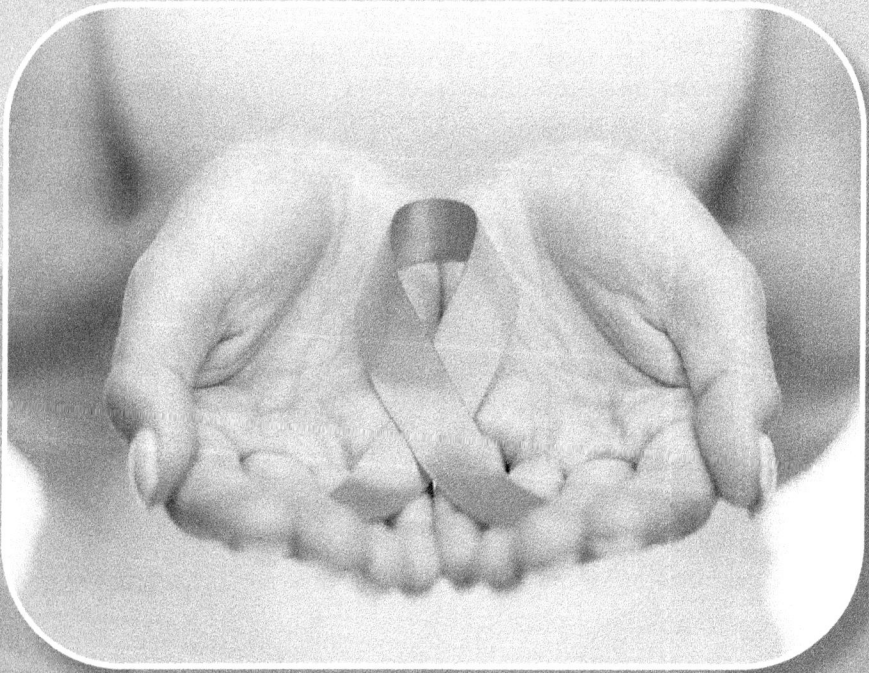

CHAPTER 2

MY AMAZING BREAST CANCER JOURNEY

I have been cancer-free for eight years, and I thank God for this healing. I was diagnosed with breast cancer on March 28, 2014. My first reactions were shock, surprise and terrible fear. I felt like everything just stopped; no one ever wants to hear the word "cancer." Suddenly, my whole world changed in front of my eyes. I remember I cried heavily in the car; I stayed there for a long time. I had a heart-to-heart talk with God, with mixed emotions. I told Him about my fears about having this sickness. After this heartfelt talk with God and crying with Him, surrendering everything to Him, I felt incredibly relieved from my worry. I experienced calmness. God was there with me in the car, reassuring me and cheering me up. Thank you, Lord!

My breast cancer battle was a true roller coaster ride, involving many emotional highs and lows, with really difficult times, not knowing what would happen next. I have always been a positive person, but dealing with cancer, I could easily get into a very dark place. It can be a worrisome feeling as well; merely deciding what procedure and treatments to take can be confusing.

But I knew that wasn't how I wanted to live my life. I chose to focus on myself and my health. I concluded, "Okay, I'll take it one step at a time and just go with what the experts have to say and recommend." Furthermore, knowing that God – the number one healer of everything – was there for me gave me the feeling of hope, with the assurance that I would be okay and would be healed from this disease.

That altered my attitude toward this illness and the whole scenario of my breast cancer journey. My mastectomy procedure and the immediate breast reconstruction were both successful. I just trusted the process, and it went very well. I was fortunate to have very good doctors who are highly knowledgeable in their fields of expertise. Likewise, my healing process was not difficult. However, in one of my chemotherapy sessions, I got a severe allergic reaction, so my chemotherapy was stopped. I wasn't certain what to feel – whether to rejoice or not – as I was having some side effects, like hammer-like pain 24-7, nausea and vomiting, and a metallic taste in my mouth that made food taste so bad.

I remember the first day that I lost my hair while I was taking a shower. Strands were coming out by the handful. I felt sad because I loved my long black hair, but then I opted to shave it off. I realized that hair was only a material thing, and it did grow back. Actually, I loved it when I was bald; I got to wear lovely wigs, scarves and bandannas. I can recall getting compliments about being bald – people saying that it was sexy and attractive – and that was flattering. Also, I have always believed that beauty comes from within, so being bald and losing a part of my body could still be a very beautiful thing.

Breast cancer is a life-changing event, and it has changed mine in such a profound way. It made me feel so loved and cared for. All of the staff – the nurses, doctors and everyone who worked in the cancer department – were all very nice. I think they must have been well-chosen and exceptionally trained for this job. Everyone was so kind to me and to all of the cancer patients who were undergoing treatments. As a matter of fact, I felt like a princess during my chemotherapy sessions, starting in the reception area while waiting for my appointment: I would be asked if I wanted coffee, tea, crackers or cookies. Afterwards, in the treatment room, I would be offered any drink that I wanted and a warm blanket and pillows. Every now and then, there would be someone roaming around, providing coffee, tea, cookies and warm blankets as well. The hospital staff and nurses kept checking on how I was doing, and I was given full attention. It made me feel really important. In effect, I always looked forward to my chemotherapy session because of the exceptional treatment they gave me. I feel that everyone being so kind-hearted, good-natured and compassionate was instrumental in my fast recovery. The world needs more people like them. Thank you to all the staff, nurses and doctors at the Surrey Memorial Hospital and British Columbia Cancer Agency. Kudos to all of you for doing a great job!

Indeed, surviving this cancer battle has been empowering. There's so much to celebrate. It offered me an amazing story of survival; it made me realize what truly matters in my life. I've been given the permission to rest, slow down and say "No" for an answer, if I deem that appropriate. Saying "No" was tough for me, so this small accomplishment is a biggie for me.

This journey has not just made me recognize how strong I am. I've also learned to truly appreciate life in very simple ways. Most of all, this battle got me closer to God, who created me. I thank God for giving me a second chance in life.

I was also fortunate that I had critical illness insurance, which helped me tremendously. It allowed me to focus on getting better and to not worry about any lost income, easing financial pressures while I was coping with my illness, particularly because I had my son, who relies on me. I can truly say that critical illness insurance is worth having.

To all of my amazing friends and family who were so supportive during my cancer fight, I want to express my sincerest thanks. I am beyond fortunate for all of your help, care and love, for your tireless and unceasing prayers and unwavering support. I love you all! For all of those who brought me to my doctor's appointments and chemotherapy treatments, I am so thankful.

And to my son, who was patient, understanding and helpful throughout my cancer journey, I'm forever grateful. There were several times that I had to miss his sports practices, games and school functions because of my sickness and the effects of chemotherapy, but he understood.

This incredible journey helped me to find strength and courage and to appreciate life in very meaningful ways. I gained friends in the chemotherapy room who just accepted who I was and cared for me. It was a very kind-hearted, loving environment. I felt the love, warmth, attention, friendliness, kindness and compassion. It's kind of sad that it takes a situation like this to realize and experience all of these wonderful things. Let's not just give tremendous love, care and respect to those who have survived, are currently fighting, or have departed from this horrible disease; but also give these things to everyone in our lives and in this world before it's too late.

As a breast cancer survivor, I'm thankful that I have another day to live and be with my son, family and friends. I've realized that every day is a bonus, and life is so precious and short. I appreciate life even more. If you have ever been down this road, you can never give back enough. I'm thankful that I can do this even in the simplest ways.

If you feel or see anything unusual in your body, do not procrastinate and wait another day to go to a doctor to have yourself checked out. I know we all have busy lives, and life happens sometimes, but we need to stop and take care of ourselves. We're working hard; we're taking care of our kids, our family and other people, so we forget to stop and say, "*Wait. Am I okay? Is anything wrong with me?*" There's nothing more important than our good health; as the saying goes, "Health is wealth." Good health is the real wealth of our life and the highest blessing, which must not be taken for granted. It can bring desired happiness, enjoyment and pleasure and can prevent us from getting any kind of sickness. Money may buy us all the luxuries in the world, but it cannot buy us good health. We are solely responsible for our own good health, and the choice is uniquely ours.

CHAPTER 3

MY BATTLE WITH DEPRESSION: THERE'S ALWAYS HOPE TO GET BETTER

Author Grace B of *www.wisdomcourageacceptance.weebly.com/blog/what-depression-feels-like* defines depression as "a mood disorder that causes a persistent feeling of sadness and loss of interest. Also called major depressive disorder or clinical depression, it affects how you feel, think and behave and can lead to a variety of emotional and physical problems."

As stated in *www.heretohelp.bc.ca/infosheet/post-traumatic-stress-disorder-and-adults*, PTSD is an anxiety disorder that can occur after a person has been through a traumatic event;

include a car collision or accident, a physical or sexual assault, long-term abuse, torture, a natural disaster and other traumatic experiences."

In 2015, I had a car accident, and I was stricken by depression and PTSD, another major illness that I never thought I would get. I was, of course, in big-time denial, but I noticed I had some of the symptoms: loss of interest or pleasure in activities I once enjoyed; feeling sad, down or having a depressed mood continually; feeling worthless or guilty; difficulty thinking, concentrating or making decisions; and experiencing mood swings and negative thoughts. Similarly, any little thing became fearful for me, and there came a point at which I isolated and detached myself from other people, including friends and family. I opted to stay home for long periods of time. Then, I got alarmed, so I sought medical help and was diagnosed with PTSD and depression.

Depression has affected every area of my life, and it can be lonely at times. Hope and motivation disappear, and I feel helpless. In some of my darkest moments, I've felt the worthlessness and hopelessness. Dealing with depression can also be scary, and there were times I wanted to give up, but I always thought of my son. Also, I realized that I am not alone; God is with me always, and there's nothing to fear or worry about. I just love this verse, my daily reminder that God is on my side: "Fear not, for I am with you; be not dismayed, for I am your God. I will strengthen you, I will help you, I will uphold you with my righteous right hand." (Isa. 41:10 NKJV) This is one great way of overcoming my depression.

Here are some ways that I have coped with my depression that have really helped. I keep a gratitude journal – a diary of things for which I'm grateful. Finding one simple thing, then finding another and still more to be thankful for and writing them down is such a wonderful feeling, and it becomes a habit. I even downloaded a gratitude app on my phone for easy access.

Gratitude increases mental strength. For years, research has shown that gratitude not only reduces stress but also may play a major role in overcoming trauma. A 2006 study published in *Behavior Research and Therapy* found that Vietnam War veterans with higher levels of gratitude experienced lower rates of PTSD.

Another helpful way to cope with depression is practicing deep breathing. Whenever the fear and the flashbacks to the accident give me anxiety, I will do deep breathing, and it sure does the magic. According to a study by Dr. Chris Streeter, "Breathing deeply is said to help anxiety and depression. Breathing deeply slows down the release of cortisol, a stress hormone, which is why there is a link between stress and breathing. Stress heightens the symptoms of anxiety and depression, which is why breathing is said to help with this."

In addition, some useful things I do are dancing, listening to beautiful and relaxing music, going for a walk, talking it out, doing my best to go to bed earlier, reminiscing about the good times and smiling more often. I had counseling as well and have regular visits with my psychiatrist.

I came across this beautiful quote, whose author is unknown: "Depression, anxiety and panic attacks are not sign of weakness. They are signs of having tried to remain strong for too long." I have opted to think of it this way; it helps me go through the journey a bit easier.

CHAPTER 4

LIFE'S GREAT LESSONS IN OVERCOMING CHALLENGES, TRIALS AND PAINS

I want to share simple ways to overcome challenges, trials and pains that have worked wonders for me and are still producing good outcomes. I intend to continue applying them as I go through my life journey. I hope these methods can help you conquer your challenges as well.

The Power of Prayers and My Work in Progress with The Lord

There was a point in my life when I was guilty of neglecting God. It was easy for me to say, *"Life happens, and my busyness stands in the way."* I thought I could do it all alone. I considered myself strong, confident and smart and thought I was built to last. Furthermore, I believed I could accomplish exceptional achievements by myself. But something happened on March 28, 2014, when I was diagnosed with breast cancer. I was stunned and terrified. Just the word "cancer" can bring about fear and worry. I wanted to believe it was not true and that this was not happening to me. I remember vividly staying in the car for a long time, praying to God, earnestly thanking Him for his unconditional love for me, asking for His forgiveness for all of the wrongdoings I had committed, and saying I was sorry that I had neglected Him in my life. I was crying hard and praying at the same time. And what a coincidence — it suddenly rained heavily! I told myself, "God truly loves me, and He must be crying with me (maybe just for my own comfort and consolation) with a matching smile."

I was afraid to tell my only son, Tyrell, and my family. But God is so good; He made things easier for me. He helped me through my whole breast cancer journey. He's there at my side at all times, in every way possible. God is my great healer. Thank you, God!

God is my hope, my strength, refuge and comfort; with all the prayers from family and friends, my breast cancer challenge became an easy ride for me. Indeed, my breast cancer journey was beautiful, though a bit challenging, with some complications and the severe allergic reaction to chemotherapy. But it has made me build a stronger personal relationship with God, and I'm so grateful for this. It's an awesome experience living my life with God. It is now my practice in every situation or decision, in every difficulty or problem, to pray to God first and seek His guidance, love and grace. I do my best not to worry but take problems to the Lord and lift it all up to Him. Every time I talk to God, I'm so happy. I tell him everything — my joys, my laughter, my wins, my falls, my stumbles, my fears, my worries — anything under the sun, for that matter — I make sure He knows it all. I surrender all things to God and always pray for His unconditional love, care and guidance. And He definitely takes care of everything. I love you, God!

My heart has established profound peace through my relationship with God, and it has transformed my life in so many wonderful ways. I know that I'm still a work in progress with the Lord, but He assures me that He loves me, and He will not leave me alone; I am so blessed. God is there to oversee and lovingly direct my path. Moreover, I'm grateful for all my family, friends and people who continuously pray for me and my son. I offer special thanks to Pastor Dan and Sister Norma and all of my brothers and sisters in Christ. They continually pray for our safety, guidance, encouragement and continued blessings. There is nothing better than other people praying for us. Prayer is powerful and one of the best gifts we can receive. There is no cost, but there are a lot of rewards. Let's pray for people that we want God to bless; never put it off or postpone it.

God is good all the time; all the time, God is good. He will make a way where there seems to be no way and makes everything possible. God's time is the best time; we just have to be patient. Isaiah 60:22 says, "When the time is right, I, the Lord, will make it happen." I used to feel an emotional void in my life, like something was missing, but now I believe that my life has a deeper meaning and a higher purpose. Nowadays, I enjoy teaching children in Sunday school; I take delight in volunteering at senior centers, where we joyously sing gospel songs — and carols at Christmastime — and talk to the seniors. What an overflowing joy and a life worth living for!

Cry It Out: A Good Release

New York Times reporter Benedict Carey referred to tears as *"emotional perspiration."* After a good cry, we always feel cleansed. He further pointed out that "tears are just one of many miracles that work so well that we take them for granted every day." Research has found that in addition to being comforting, shedding tears releases oxytocin and endorphins. These chemicals make people feel good and may also relieve both physical and emotional pain. Thus, crying can help reduce pain and promote a sense of well-being."

Crying is one of the healthiest mechanisms I use to cope with my emotions. When I cry, I release negative tension that builds up from my day-to-day existence, allowing me to feel comforted and recharged, so I can pick myself back up afterward. Crying is my stress reliever; it lifts my spirit and makes me feel better. My tears are an expression for any kind of emotions I have. Crying is my go to. When I'm angry, stressed-out, upset or deeply troubled, I cry my heart out while praying to God wholeheartedly. After that, I'm so relieved and relaxed, and then I smile.

Do Whatever It Takes, Do Not Quit and Never Give Up

Life is about failing and learning from our mistakes. If we want a truly happy and successful life, we have to be willing to stand up, never give up and just do whatever it takes. As stated in *www.businessinsider.com/11-inspirational-quotes-that-will-supercharge-your-day-2011-6,* "Truly successful people are positive, and they know that each failure gets them closer to their goals."

With all of my life's struggles, most days I want to give up, especially in my battle with depression; I just want to end the suffering. But then I think of my son, my family – and I pray to God sincerely to control my mind and strengthen my heart. And I thank God; I never give up. Like with this book: I started writing it a few years ago, but then when depression hit me, I lost my motivation to continue writing; I had difficulty thinking and concentrating. However, I'm so determined and hopeful about finishing it. Definitely, perseverance and determination play a big role, and the hope that dwells in my heart helps me to never give up.

We must never give up on our lives and dreams. No matter how many times we get knocked down, let's find the courage to bounce back. As long as we are alive, everything is possible.

It's All about the Bounce Back: The Power of Resilience

An article in the June 9, 2020 issue of *Psychology Today* indicated that "bouncing back is what we do when we face disappointment, defeat and failure, but instead of wallowing or letting things keep us down; we get back up and continue on with our lives." In *www.mindtools.com/pages/article/resilience.htm*, "resilience is the ability to withstand adversity and bounce back from difficult life events. Resilient people don't dwell on failures; they acknowledge the situation, learn from their mistakes and then move forward."

Furthermore, *www.mindtools.com/pages/article/resilience.htm* states that "the beauty of it is that resilience is not an inborn personality trait that some people naturally have and others lack. It's a learned skill that involves behaviors, thoughts and actions that can be learned and developed in anyone as we age. And that's good news, because being resilient is one of the best ways to protect against the effects of stress and adversity."

Resilience is important for various reasons: It gives people the strength they need to process and overcome hardships; it can also protect us from the development of some mental health difficulties and concerns, and it enables us to develop techniques to overcome challenges and work through problems. Flexibility, staying optimistic and not blaming ourselves are essential parts of resilience. Let's be kinder to ourselves. It's important to be empathetic, not just to others, but to ourselves. As confirmed in *www.mindtools.com/pages/article/resilience.htm*, "Resilient people also never think of themselves as victims; they focus their time and energy on changing the things that they have control over."

I have undergone quite a few adversities in life; resilience is the one quality that got me through difficult times. The key is resilience: our ability to bounce back after big setbacks and live with joy and purpose. And one thing is for sure, the comeback is always stronger than the setback.

It's All about the Mindset: Life Is Only as Good as Your Mindset

In his book, *Wealth for All: Living a Life of Success at the Edge of Your Ability*, Idowu Koyenikan writes, "The mind is just like a muscle – the more you exercise it, the stronger it gets and the more it can expand." He further states that "The mind has a powerful way of attracting things that are in harmony with it, good and bad." Very true, because what we think about and focus on expands. If we concentrate on negativity, it can lead to all sorts of unpleasant stuff, including anxiety, stress, fear, depression and discouragement. However, if we direct our minds to positive thinking, it can result to lower rates of depression, distress and better psychological and physical well-being.

Courtney E. Ackerman of *www.positivepsychology.com/team/ courtney-acker* concluded that "Positive thinking is a mental and emotional attitude that focuses on the bright side of life and expects positive results. Having a positive mindset means making positive thinking a habit, continually searching for the silver lining and making the best out of any situation you find yourself in." And as cited by Jemi Sudhakar of *www.linkedin. com/pulse/hold-your-positive-spirit-powerful-ms-jemi-sudhakar;* "This is quite important, as it helps you to cope more easily with the daily affairs of life. It brings optimism into your life and makes it easier to avoid worries and negative thinking."

Over the years, I have done my best to have a positive mindset. I continuously attend personal growth development courses and events to further improve my positive and effective life choices and decisions and to enable personal empowerment as well. I make a conscious effort to start my day with a positive affirmation. I talk to myself in front of the mirror, and this alone puts a smile on my face, as I make fun of myself, and it feels silly sometimes. I will say, "I'm beautiful, I'm awesome and I'm going to have a fabulous day!" It definitely has a great impact on me and how my day goes.

Similarly, I focus on the good in things and in people, find humor in bad situations and turn failures into lessons or opportunities. Also, I'm always thankful for everything and everyone, most especially God. There is something so powerful about being grateful. It immediately nourishes my soul and changes everything. Furthermore, I engage in random acts of kindness, like cooking for a friend, paying for the next person in line, giving someone a compliment and many other things. It can be so simple and easy, but the optimism that it creates and the benefits are remarkable and almost endless.

These are just some effortless things out of the countless things that have contributed to my having a positive mindset, and I aspire to do more. As basketball coach Pat Riley said, "If you have a positive attitude and constantly strive to give your best effort, eventually you will overcome your immediate problems and find you are ready for greater challenges."

Turn Challenges, Trials and Pains into Opportunities

We are all faced with challenges throughout our lives, and challenges come in all shapes and sizes. How we look at things and how we show up varies and can make a huge difference. It has become my practice that with every obstacle, I look for the opportunity, the good lessons and benefits that I can apply for my personal growth. Being open, accepting things as they are and being ready to move on are some of the best ways to transform challenges, trials and pains into opportunities. These have worked very well for me, and I'm continuously implementing them. Failures in life are merely turning points and can be useful in one's progress and advancement in life. And it's up to us how to implement the lessons learned and take the proper steps that will get us closer to our goals. As confirmed in *www.carolynjrivera.com/turning-challenges-into-opportunities,* "If we train our minds to see things differently, we're giving ourselves a chance to succeed."

I remember when the new principal of the college I worked for laid me off. She said that my job position had been eliminated due to reorganization. I felt so devastated; I loved my job, and the student body loved me as well. In fact, I had been given an award for exemplary work. Being laid off can be an overwhelming and stressful experience of loss and change. It had a significant emotional impact on me. I just stayed home and didn't want to go out, cried all the time and lost my confidence. However, very good news happened: Professors connected with me and informed me that the principal had posted a job notice for the same position. They told me to pursue this matter further, so I presented my case to several lawyers, but apparently, because I was given a separation package, my case was in a grey area, and they would not work on a contingency basis.

It was burdensome, as I did not have the money to pay a lawyer, but I did not give up. One lawyer advised me to write a very strong letter, detailing what had happened, and to send it to the president. If nothing happened, the lawyer said he would represent me on a contingency basis. But God is so good: the president replied to my letter and flew in to meet with me. I got an excellent offer, and he fired the principal for having given me a wrongful dismissal. I jumped for joy, regained my confidence and moved on with my life.

I'm grateful for this learning experience, as it influences my job choices and decision-making, I successfully ended up in a sales career that offers limitless earning potential, gives personal satisfaction and provides professional growth.

Other ways to overcome challenges, trials and pains that greatly help me in my journey are as follows:

- Develop an Attitude of Gratitude (Practice Random Acts of Kindness)

- Believe in Yourself: Be the Best Version of Yourself

- Learn How to Be Courageous and Persistent

- Stand Tall, Be True to Yourself and Speak Your Truth

- Let It Go and Get Over It

- Forgive Others for Your Inner Peace

- Have a Great Support System – Appreciate the Gift of Family, Friendship and Relationships

- Embrace Challenges as Opportunities

- Ha! Ha! Ha! Laughter is the Best Medicine

- It's Okay Not to Be Okay; No One Is Perfect

- Nurture the Powers of Compassion, Creativity and Resilience

- Stop, Look and Listen to the Inner Voice Within

- Breathe in, Breathe out and Stop to Smell the Roses

- Stay in Your Lane and Refrain from Judging Others

- Take Action! Go Big, Go Bigger or Go Home

- Think Big and Outside the Box

- Utilize the Powers of Choice, Focus, Determination, Commitment and Decision-Making

- Take a Break: Unplug from Social Media

- Pay Attention to This Word – "Can't" – and Replace It with "Can"

- Declutter Your Mind and Your Space: Unwind Better

CHAPTER 5

THE POWER OF 26

According to *www.sunsigns.org/angel-number-26-meaning*, "the number 26 in numerology symbolizes realism, family, business, teamwork, diplomacy as well as efficiency. It also depicts happiness, sorrows, joys and hardship. This further encourages us to maintain a positive outlook on things." That's why I chose number 26. It represents the 26 letters of the alphabet – which I called the A to Zen of life wherein each letter has meaning in my purposeful life. In Dalai Lama's wise and powerful ideas, *A* means to *Avoid* negative sources, people, places, things and habits. *Z* stands for *Zero in* on your target and go for it; to name a few meaning of the alphabet.

The Power of 26 consists of 26 people whose real-life stories have inspired many people. They are continually making a difference and impacting people's lives. These are also people who have affected and greatly influenced my life. For this book, they discussed their precious lives, their failures, their stumbles, their falls and their wins. They shared the true life lessons they have learned throughout their lives.

I would like to take this opportunity to congratulate each of **you** for being chosen as one of the Top 26 people in this signature and exclusive portion of my book.

It is my great pride and honor to share your inspiring and amazing life stories. I hope that they will be a motivation and encouragement to many people.

Bernard Dalziel

I was dyslexic, which made school a challenge, and I was ready to quit at age 12. Yet there were moments and individuals that helped me during this academic struggle. Then I started down a self-destructive path, one that led to alcohol, smoking and drugs. It was a way of life that could have cost me mine. Just as I seemed determined to follow this path of self-destruction, when I was 15, I lost my father.

As I got closer to age 16, I realized that I needed to be a man. I had to stop doing drugs because I had to step up and help my mother. It was time for me to grow up. I truly started to take control of my life and shape it to fit my vision, instead of allowing others' opinions of my capabilities to define me. No longer did I see myself as an academic failure, but as someone with unique gifts and talents that I could share with others.

With all of my life's struggles, I learned to trust Jesus and that through Him, all things are possible. I thank God for His help, wisdom and guidance. I believe that God has a plan for me and for everyone, and God's plan is always the best.

A Personal Glimpse of Bernard

Bernard H. Dalziel graduated in 1979 from Victoria High School, Victoria, British Columbia. He started apprenticeship at the *Vancouver Sun* and *The Province* in the post-press department and worked there for a long time.

He has taken several personal development courses with Raymond Aaron, including monthly mentoring. In fact, he graduated and co-authored *The Book of Authorities – How To Do IOAL (Income, Out of Wealth Expenses (OWE), Assets and Liabilities), A Simple Financial Blueprint* with co-authors Les Brown, Raymond Aaron, Marci Shimoff, and Dr. Nido Qubein.

Bernard decided to dedicate his life to helping others to help themselves by providing easy-to-understand information. One area in particular where he knew he could assist was by creating a simple formula that gives people a way to create a written financial plan or blueprint. It was meant to help them change the way they think about their finances and give them an easy step-by-step process to gain financial freedom and independence. He holds a mutual funds license as well.

Bernard loves volunteering with several mental health societies in Vancouver. He is a proud grandfather to a beautiful granddaughter, Freya Georgiana. He also speaks highly of his mom, Irene, who was a very impressive individual: one who raised her children with a sense of purpose and a desire to learn. "Even to this day, she is active, and her routine could wear me out," Bernard expressed. She taught me that common sense is not that common these days. At the ripe age of 89, she takes no pills, just nutritional supplements, and leads a water aerobics class six days a week. Her one day off is for God, and she knows that God answers all who take a knee.

Bernard believes that if the elevator for success no longer works for you, then you must be able to take the stairs, one step at a time. Most people don't plan to fail; they just fail to plan.

Billy Tugano

One of the most difficult struggles that I had been through in life was when I was dismissed from my job. It was very tough because I was raising a family. I had five children. I was worried because of the loss of my normal income and feeling grief and deep anxiety that I might not be able to pay for all of the expenses and academic concerns for the children, as well.

Then, I put up my own business, which is in the packaging industry. During these hard times, I just focused on my business. I worked day and night, nonstop. My family and my dream of becoming successful were my motivation. I believed that my dream wouldn't become a reality in an instant and that there are no shortcuts in life; it takes sweat, determination and hard work.

I implemented a *"God-first"* policy in my life. I put God at the center of my life, getting involved in various Christian and religious organizations. Any trials and problems that I encounter, I just seek God's kingdom first. With His guidance, everything goes very well. I've learned that anything in life can be achieved through hard work and effort, patience, persistence and strong faith in God.

A Personal Glimpse of Billy

Billy Tugano is a retired businessman. He is the eldest of seven siblings. He finished a bachelor of science (BS) degree in business administration, supporting his education by doing different kinds of jobs, from waiter and bartender to checker and chief cashier. He worked in a big packaging company but lost his job in 1990. In the same year, he built his own packaging company, Silver Star Resources Company, Inc. With a strong faith in God, belief in his dreams, persistence and good work habits, Billy's initially small company became very successful. He went on to own four companies that employ about 800 people.

Billy presently enjoys his retirement; he loves travelling and seeing the world. He also spends quality time with his twelve grandchildren. He still is the chairman and CEO of Silver Star Resources Company, Inc. and performs consultancy for all of the companies he had built and owned.

As Billy mentioned above, he considers a key factor in his huge, continuous success to be implementing his so-called God-first policy. Every Monday and Saturday, there's a prayer meeting for all of the staff and the management team for one hour, and it's a paid attendance. They gather all together, praise God and pray together.

Dr. Neneng Galanto

The hardest struggle in my life was with failed relationships. I dreamed of being a wife and mother when I was young, but my dream turned into a nightmare. I was engaged three times, but all my smart, good-looking princes turned into frogs. The men who became my boyfriends were attractive and very helpful – to other women – and the first one impregnated another woman; I was forced to break up with him, and the other two were also lured away by other women.

I overcame this by proving to my ex-boyfriends that they had made a big mistake! Instead of crying over spilled milk, I made a decision to focus my time on serving the Lord, my savior, and by taking one course after another. I love studying my lessons, and I always strive to reach perfection. When I was about to complete my doctorate, I announced to my co-teachers that I was changing my status. My colleagues were so excited and asked who the lucky man was; my answer was, "I am not changing my status from Miss to Mrs., but from Miss to Doctor." Instead of marrying a man, I decided to marry my profession and consider my students to be my children.

The most valuable lesson for me was learning to become *"better instead of bitter"* when facing challenging circumstances in life. I believe what the Bible states in Romans 8:28: "All things work together for good to them who love God." My broken-heart experiences have become a great blessing to others who have come into contact with me. I was able to encourage many clients, when I was working as a career and employment counselor – to have hope despite their difficult situations due to broken relationships and to make their challenges an inspiration to excel.

A Personal Glimpse of Neneng

Dr. Neneng Galanto is a graduate of many different colleges and universities. She is an alumna of Central Philippine University and West Visayas State University in the Philippines, and in Canada, she is an alumna of Simon Fraser University; Kwantlen Polytechnic University; Douglas College; Vancouver Community College; Progressive Intercultural Community Services' BEST Program; National Association of Career Colleges; and the former Career College in Calgary. She has a doctorate degree in education, a master's degree in health education, a bachelor's degree in elementary education, a TESOL (Teaching English to Speakers of Other Languages) diploma, a geriatric activity coordinator certificate, a career development practitioner certificate and many others. She is a "professional student," and she desires to set a good example to her own students.

Neneng graduated as her class's valedictorian in elementary and high school and in her short-term course in Canada. She also got an average mark of 98.33% when she upgraded her instructor's course. She graduated from university as an honor student, and she was offered a teaching job right after that.

Neneng always inspires her students to do their best when they are studying. She copies the words of her late mentor, Vice Mayor Galanto, who told her there is always room at the top. Helping students to excel is her greatest passion. She was already able to work as a college administrator, but she stepped down and enjoys being a classroom instructor. She is very pleased to know that many of her graduates became model employees in Canada.

Despite her busy schedule as a college instructor, Neneng still gets involved in community activities. She is a member of the board of directors of Central Philippine University Alumni Association and the adviser of the CPUAA Alumni Association. She calls herself a "bookworm" and is a volunteer librarian at Johnston Heights Evangelical Church. She was the first auditor of FCSS, which is now called the Multicultural Helping House. She sings in the Christmas choir and runs around to help people who are in need. Sometimes, you can find her speaking to panhandlers; once, she was able to encourage a panhandler to find a job, and that person was very grateful to her.

Evelyn Miranda

When I was 50 years old, I was diagnosed with breast cancer. Luckily, it was at the early stage. I was working in one of the biggest publishing companies in the Philippines as an ad taker/ encoder. During my annual checkup, I was shocked when my physician told me that I had breast cancer. That was the hardest trial I've gone through in my entire life.

My lump was removed, and I underwent chemotherapy sessions. I prayed and asked to be healed. I surrendered my life and soul to God and asked for His forgiveness. I needed to survive because of my family and my son, whom I was supporting. After the last session of my chemotherapy, my doctor told me that I was cancer-free. I cried so much. I am grateful and blessed that God gave me another chance to live.

In every crisis that comes my way, I just pray to God, and He gives me peace, comfort and immense relief. I know He loves me unconditionally and will be there for me and will never leave me alone. Praise you, Lord! I want to share this beautiful scripture that helps me keep going in life, "Trust in the Lord with all your heart and lean not on your own understanding; in all your ways acknowledge Him, and He will make your paths straight." (Prov. 3:5–6 NIV)

A Personal Glimpse of Evelyn

Evelyn M. Miranda is 61 years old and happily retired. She worked at a major publishing company as an ad taker/encoder. She had a wonderful, 28-year experience in the field of advertising. She loves to play tennis and volleyball.

Evelyn has one son, Raymond, who has a family of his own with two beautiful children. Being a single mom, while working full-time and raising her son, was very difficult. There were moments when she almost gave up, but her strong faith in God provides her with inner strength to get through all her challenges in life. Faith gives her hope and is a source of her peace and joy.

Evelyn enjoys Zumba and is a member of a Zumba dance club. She spends her free time at a family farm and enjoys gardening. She loves to be around trees or viewing scenes of nature, as it makes her feel so relaxed, reduces anger and stress and has other health benefits. She also enjoys an early morning walk, as she believes it helps to get her blood flowing and increases alertness first thing in the morning, and that is carried throughout the day.

Gem Thater

I was 24 years old when I fell in love, hard and I gave birth to my first son when I was 25. I was 26 when another angel came, but I was broken-hearted when the father of my two beautiful kids ran off with another woman. At age 26, I became a single mom. Where I came from, it's taboo to have children without a father living under one roof. My country, the Philippines, which is predominantly Catholic, is a place where single moms are scrutinized, judged and looked down on. Where I hail from, a person with a tarnished past becomes the talk of the town and is ostracized.

This judgement led me to feel that I was never good enough and that something was awfully wrong with me. I doubted myself, and with my self-esteem eroding, I told myself that my way out would be to perish. I grabbed a knife and was about to end my life; the man who brought me into this horrible darkness was the same man who saved my life: my ex He took the knife away and I lived.

Not everybody is lucky enough to have family that cares about them, but I know I do. They are the reason that I'm still here and that my children still have their mother. The support I got from my family was immense; it moved me. The unconditional love – loving without bounds – the care and the affection they showed me have been instrumental to overcoming my obstacles.

I believe that I will overcome, and I believe that I matter in life. Believing is key. All will be well. Claim it.

A Personal Glimpse of Gem

Gem Anguluan Thater finished her bachelor's degree in journalism, and she works in the cruise line industry for Holland America line as a buyer for the supply chain since 2003. She loves going to concerts, watching Broadway shows and movies and taking road trips. She also has a passion for interior decorating and shopping. She enjoys watching football games, especially her favorite team, the Seahawks.

There's nothing else that thrills her and her husband of 23 years more than sharing delightful moments with their two cute grandchildren, whom she adoringly spoils.

Gertie Leano

Life was never good to me growing up. I experienced the worst, and it was not easy. I was young and stupid and made a lot of mistakes. It was a bad – and at the same time good – experience that made me a better person today.

I failed, but I learned to get up, adapt quickly, and keep on moving. I did not blame anyone but myself. That was the path that I chose when I was lost. My bad experiences made me strong and solid as a rock. Now, I don't need to prove myself to anyone but me.

Through my life's journey, I have learned to never give up. I continue finding the best version of myself. I didn't get mad at anybody who tried to belittle or insult me, or those who told me that I was a "nobody" and wouldn't have a future. Instead, that inspired me to keep on going in order to achieve my goals.

Believing in myself played a big role in my life. I learned and believe that I can accomplish anything that I set my mind to. The only limits are those that I impose upon myself. I can definitely do anything I set my mind to; it takes action, perseverance, facing my fears and, most likely, getting out of my comfort zone, but nothing worth having comes easily in life.

A Personal Glimpse of Gertie

Gertie Leano is a top-performing software and services sales professional with over 10 years sales and channel management experience. She received her BS degree in the Philippines and at the University of California, Irvine. Gertie is self-motivated, hardworking and possesses a high degree of professional integrity. She is ambitious and skilled in applying a logical, common sense approach to seeking practical solutions. Since childhood, she has possessed the mindset of what Kobe Bryant was well known for – the *"mamba mentality"* – as she is constantly seeking to be the best version of herself. Gertie is known to have a very strong personality but also a big heart. She does not give up easily and turns any obstacle into an opportunity.

Gertie volunteers at Hire Heroes USA, where she encourages US military members, veterans and military spouses to succeed in the civilian workforce by conducting mock interviews.

Gina Pinangat

Belonging... The need to belong has always been most important for me as I've gone on with life. As a Filipino-Canadian, I wanted to be accepted and to be one with my colleagues, friends and be part of a diverse culture, race and tradition and as a part of the Canadian mosaic.

Beingness is who we are at the very core of life, and as we live out of our beingness, we will find life to be so much more fun and fulfilling. Appreciate life, express love, show gratitude and practice abundance are also some valuable lessons that I live by.

I want to share my favorite quote from Ralph Marston "Make it a habit to tell people thank you. To express your appreciation, sincerely and without the expectation of anything in return. Truly appreciate those around you, and you'll soon find many others around you. Truly appreciate life, and you'll find that you have more of it."

A Personal Glimpse of Gina

Her name is **Gina Pinangat**. She arrived in Montreal as a live-in caregiver and housekeeper under the Foreign Domestic Movement program in 1991. After receiving her immigrant status, she took some college courses while working as a cleaner for her boss and her boss's friend. Gina never stopped striving and took some university courses to further her education. She was one of the few Filipino-Canadians who worked for the now-defunct Nortel Networks Corporation. She was handpicked by her boss to attend a company-sponsored program in telecommunications and was the only female who graduated, out of the many hundreds of starters. She was blessed to have made a decision to finish the program, as she was laid off from Nortel in her last year in the program.

Gina enlisted to the Canadian Armed Forces in 2003. This veteran was as an aerospace telecommunications and information systems technician with a specialization in communications systems maintenance and repair. She has a college diploma in telecommunications from the Institute Teccart in Montreal. She prequalified in the direct entry program of the Canadian Forces, which was offered at the time of recruitment. Upon completion of basic military training, she was awarded the rank of corporal. In December 2006, she was fully trained at the Canadian Forces School of Communications and Electronics and qualified to maintain and repair the military aerospace and communications systems. She trained new and incoming technicians on the MACS system as well. She was a military co-chair of the Defense Visible Minority and Advisory Group at the CFB Esquimalt in 2006 and 2007.

Janeth Anguluan

I believe that the hardest struggle I've been through was in October of 2015, when my husband of almost 25 years succumbed to a massive heart attack. Little did I know that fateful night would be the last time that I would see him. In my heart and mind, I believed that after an emergency room visit, he would either be confined for a few days, or better yet, after a few hours in the ER, we would bring him home, and it would be "normal programming" for my children, Baham, who was seventeen at that time, Yani, who was eight, and me.

As I entered the ER, a nurse supervisor approached immediately and asked me if I was sure I wanted to see my husband, who was in a very bad condition; I clearly remember my reply to her: "I need to see him."

That was the longest night of my life, and when the doctor pronounced my husband's time of death, my whole body was numb. There were a lot of things going on in my mind: What would happen to my kids? In the blink of an eye, they were fatherless. In hindsight, I feel especially sorry for my Yani, whose dancing partner was gone. Who would dance with her on her eighteenth birthday? On her wedding day? To this day, there's a lump in my throat, and a big sword pierces my heart when it crosses my mind. What would happen to us? My kids were so used to their dad being around. He was the one volunteering for their school activities, and he was their number-one ally, because I was the bad cop in the family. How I wished he was only on vacation, at a Masonic convention or on a weekend trip, but no – he was gone. He was gone forever and would never come back.

Overcoming the loss of a loved one is very difficult and an overwhelming challenge. . Though it's mushy and an old cliché, the pain is always there; you cannot forget the pain. Life has to go on, but a part of me was still living in the time before that fateful night, when everything was still complete. How could anyone move on? That was easier said than done. I needed to live for my kids; I needed to work even harder for them and for my sanity.

Family, friends who became our family and my husband's brother Masons filled the gap left in his absence. Life is a journey. I just needed to enjoy the ride and get a clearer view.

My faith tells me that I have a bigger God than the challenges that have been thrown at me in the past and right now. I've been to worst situations in my life and come back repeatedly, with a smile on my face, not asking why things are not going how I wanted them to go. God has His own way of presenting things to me that are better – if not the best – for me and my kids. With what I have been through, what else is there that I cannot handle?

A Personal Glimpse of Janeth

Janeth Cruz Anguluan is the proud mom of Baham, Yani and Aubrey and is "Mamu" to her three-year-old grandson, Emmett. She lives in Orange County, California in the USA. She is an advocate of positivity, and her love for her parents, siblings and their families and her genuine character have molded the person she is today.

John Edwards

My hardest struggle was in 2001, when I had several major events occur within a four-month period. Firstly, my mother passed away on July 6, the day of my oldest sister's birthday. Secondly, on September 4, two days after returning from a family holiday, my wife announced that she was seeking a divorce. Then, exactly one week later, 9/11 happened on the day of my birthday, and finally, in October, my company announced that I was one of several senior managers who were being let go.

Through the support of my family and trusted friends and, of course, through prayers, I was able to overcome all of these challenges in my life. The most valuable lesson that I learned is that life is short, and every moment should be cherished.

A Personal Glimpse of John

John Edwards is a Canadian who was born in Barbados. He lived and studied nursing in England and then moved to Canada to work for the Government of British Columbia in the healthcare sector. After four years in healthcare, he changed careers to work for a Merck subsidiary and other global pharmaceutical companies in sales and management positions. In 2005, John made another career change by joining a US medical device company. He finished his career as a senior director responsible for global sales, and he visited several countries as part of his job.

John dabbled in federal and city politics; he unsuccessfully contested the mayoral position in Surrey, BC in 2014. Since 2010, he has been a member of the Rotary Club of Surrey, where he served as president for three one-year terms. He also served as the Canadian membership co-chair for District 5050.

John loves travelling and seeing the world. He also enjoys supporting various non-profit projects and volunteering, as it allows him to connect to the community and make it a better place to live.

Joji Lassam

The hardest struggle I had been through in life was when my marriage broke down and my family fell apart. It was the lowest point in my life because it happened when I had just arrived in Canada, and my family and I were in the midst of settling into a new place and an entirely new environment. I thought we had a whole lifetime to spend together, but unexpectedly, it turned out to be the other way around. The realization that my marriage was over was like coming face-to-face with a horrifying, and yet entirely predictable, demon.

My children and I fell into very difficult times that tested our spirits and stretched our resolve. Losing my marriage felt like I was without a purpose, like I had permanently and irrevocably failed at the single most important thing in my life.

My marriage was not ideal, but you could say love abounds in our family. I am blessed to have come from a family with very strong support and unfailing love. My shortcomings, on hindsight, have become a blessing in disguise, for in my most challenging times; love emerged from the family that taught me to be kinder, more giving and more understanding.

"Those who fly solo have the strongest wings." - Author Unknown.

As a single parent, I would readily agree. But the wind beneath my wings is blown by the love and assurances – consistent, persistent and unfailing – from the big family that I have by God's grace and faithfulness.

The most valuable lesson I have learned is to continue growing in love, faith and trust in God. God should be in the midst of every aspect of the relationship, so when challenges come, by God's grace, relationship issues can be dealt with accordingly, without negative feelings and emotions on the surface, such as pride, anger, doubt, fear, and the like. They are but the causes of couples ending up separated and divorced and families breaking apart.

A Personal Glimpse of Joji

Joji Lassam is a single parent of three boys. She works as a healthcare assistant at Cedarview Lodge. She graduated with a bachelor's degree in psychology from University of Santo Tomas (UST). She is a member of Handmaids of the Lord. Joji is actively involved in the UST Alumni Association and organizes dinner dance galas, wherein the various contributions of the UST alumni in British Columbia that impact others are recognized. She participates in her parish as a Catholic Women's League member, working with other women to promote Catholic values and to carry out volunteer and charitable work.

Her advocacy is helping poor but deserving students to pursue higher education.

Joven Magcawas

During the time when my wife worked as an accountant in a reputable government agency, and I was delivering branded medicines with the help of my brother and sister; our life was stable. Then, my wife left to work abroad hoping to sustain the needs of our growing family, especially the education of our children. It was difficult to be away from each other, especially for the children; no one can replace the presence of a mother. We went through a lot of relationship pressures and feeling lonely. I had to fight all these emotions and keep moving forward for the sake of our children.

The funds coming in were unpredictable and insufficient to accommodate all the expenses. That's why I made the wise decision to find another means of livelihood, which was farming.

In farming, I can say that I can reap the bearing fruits abundantly, but sometimes, due to some climatic disturbances, like typhoons, plants are ruined. I never surrendered; instead, I continued learning about the significance of farming. I also attended seminars sponsored by the Department of Agriculture at University of the Philippines, Los Baños that eventually boosted my morale and gave me confidence.

In my life's journey, I've realized to never give up and to focus on whatever deeds I can do for the goodness of the entire family. Likewise, trust in God is very important in dealing with life's adversities.

A Personal Glimpse of Joven

Joven L. Magcawas is 52 years of age, and he is married with four children. He's thankful to God that all of them turned out to be wonderful; he considers his children to be his precious jewels, whom he will treasure all his life. He loves them dearly.

Presently, Joven is engaged in the farming business, which he believes creates opportunities to lift people out of poverty and can be a good source of income. He is also passionate about raising goats. He's convinced that raising them can help his family to achieve a sustainable lifestyle, as they are one of the most versatile animals one can own.

No matter how many challenges and trials Joven has encountered, he faces them with a positive attitude and moves ahead with life. He believes in always praying, never giving up, accepting failures willingly and learning from them.

Julieta Dioquino

The hardest struggle that I have been through in my life was when I was working in a prestigious company, and I experienced verbal harassment and bullying. I thought to myself, "How can anyone bully an adult?" The sad reality is, people can be bullied at any age and in any situation. I had been humiliated in front of colleagues and was constantly picked on, plus my views and opinions were being ignored. I also experienced verbal abuse, which was very damaging and caused me emotional harm. I did keep a private record documenting everything – the dates and times, the people involved, exactly what they were doing and saying. I took it to my manager and to the human resources department, but to no avail.

In times like those, prayer has been my most powerful weapon. I am most resilient and determined to take action and prove my worth; especially knowing that Jesus is always there for me and will never abandon me.

My well-being is most important; I did all I could to end the bullying, but it was still occurring, so I decided to leave the company. It's time for me to explore other options. Through this journey, I have learned to forgive. I asked God to help me forgive those people who had hurt me and to send them blessings and healing also, wherever they might need it in their lives. I also focused on the lessons I had learned, not on the pains. I know that every difficult situation can be a learning opportunity.

A Personal Glimpse of Julieta

Julieta M. Dioquino graduated with a Bachelor of Arts (BA) degree in business administration, with a major in management. She has completed legal secretarial and community health programs with honors in Canada.

She is a member of Community for Christ Foundation for Family and Life. She has done volunteer work for various non-profit organizations. She wishes to be a part of the Live Christ Share Christ movement in the Philippines, especially in the area where she grew up and spent her childhood. She has three beautiful children and a loving husband. She loves traveling and exploring the world.

Julieta is the kind of person who is always willing to help, give and love unconditionally. She is a selfless woman who's always concerned with the needs and wishes of others and doing things for others without expecting anything in return. She believes her faith in God makes her a stronger person; no matter what comes her way, she'll conquer it. Her encouragement and her gift of friendship and wisdom that she continuously shares with all of the people around her are remarkable.

Leila Magcawas

For so many years of our harmonious marriage, we enjoyed life to the fullest, but then my husband suddenly got sick of cancer and died. This was a big shock to me and my family. Instantly, I became a single mom of four children. It was not easy, but I did not lose hope and instead became a brave, patient and strong woman for my children. The hardest part of being a stay-at-home mom is that it is a continuous job – 24/7. No other job in the world requires as much on-duty time as a stay-at-home mom, but it is very gratifying.

The struggles and challenges of being a single mom – from self-doubt and anxiety over money to the stress of making decisions alone – can be overwhelming, but I am so thankful to my family for all of their help and support. They gave me financial help to put up a business distributing drugs to hospitals, clinics and drugstores. After a couple of years, the business became profitable, which sustained the needs of my entire family.

In my life's journey, I have learned to be courageous and steadfast and to persevere. I emphasize the importance of saving money for the betterment of the future, and I believe there's always hope.

A Personal Glimpse of Leila

Leila Magcawas graduated with a BS degree in business administration from the University of Manila. She also finished a secretarial course in Laguna, Philippines. She supported herself while studying by working in an office near the university, then was employed by a big company, where she met a wonderful man named Angel. After being engaged for three years, they got married and have four children.

Unfortunately, the company Leila worked for collapsed during the Philippine economic downturn in the early 1980s and permanently closed. Her husband then took employment abroad to support the family. Life was good: Leila became a stay-at-home mom and gave up her career to nurture her children day in and day out, while her husband supported the family. Being with her children throughout the day and taking care of their needs gave her immense satisfaction. She cherished all the precious moments with them. She is so proud of the kind of people all of her wonderful children have become.

Leila is now happily retired, loves Zumba and reconnecting with all her friends, classmates and batch mates. They often have get-togethers and picnics, and just share laughter while reminiscing about beautiful memories and creating precious moments. She's a fun-loving person and that definitely shows in her physical appearance: She looks way younger than her age. She said people call her an *"ageless beauty."*

Lina Dichoso

The hardest struggle in my life was when I became a single mom at age 23; my life was so tough. Some people underestimated me because of my situation. I thought the world had stopped; there was a lot of blaming myself, guilt, emotional challenges and financial strain and responsibility. I needed to be strong for my dearest child. I prayed and asked God to have my family forgive me. I continuously prayed for more strength, courage and wisdom to think and act righteously. No matter how painful my situation was, I had to fight and to face life the best way I could.

The most valuable thing is I've learned to obtain a state of enlightenment and to have a realization. After all those trials and challenges, I won't be pushed around by the fears and worries in my mind. Instead of worrying about what I cannot control, I have to shift my energy into something productive and beneficial. I should not dwell in the past or worry about the future but should focus on living fully in the present. I have also learned to embrace all pains and challenges in order to live a successful, happy life. I have to push myself beyond what I can currently accomplish, so I can achieve greater things tomorrow.

Finally, I learned to put God at the center of my life. In everything, He is my strength and savior. He is there and protects me from any harm and difficulties, and I have genuine joy, even in adverse moments.

A Personal Glimpse of Lina

Lina Magcawas Dichoso is 57 years old. She was born in the beautiful city of Seven Lakes, San Pablo, Laguna, Philippines. She is married to Dicherson Dichoso and is blessed with four wonderful children: Kaye, Lawrence, Yna Marielle and Dana.

Lina has seven siblings; her parents raised them to be God-fearing, kind and honest people. Being poor, in turn, led her to strive harder and pursue her studies. She graduated with a bachelor of commerce degree (major in accountancy). She believes that God has never failed her in all of her challenges. All of her prayers have been answered. God gave her a man who accepted her past and uplifted her whole being as a woman.

Lina did her best to give her family a good future. She started work as a clerk, then as a secretary, and now she is a legislative staff officer in the House of Representatives. She has an entrepreneurial spirit and has successfully created businesses despite her busy schedule. She has worked doubly hard for her family.

Lina believes her family, especially her parents, would be proud of her now, as she is a *"black sheep transformed into a better mom."* The greatest achievement of her life would be seeing her children with a happy, peaceful and stable life. It cannot be measured by power, success and any material things in this world. Her children are everything to her: her inspiration and her life. It is her fervent hope that the way her parents brought her and her siblings up will be a guide for Lina's children, so they will be more courageous and stronger to face every storm of life today and tomorrow.

Lina is an amazing woman, beautiful inside and out, who continues to stand strong, despite all of the obstacles in her life. When she falls down, she gets right back up and keeps moving forward.

Maidee Mabale

Being away from my family was my life from 1994 until now. It is very hard, but I need to pursue my dream to help my parents while they are still alive. Being an Overseas Filipino Worker (OFW) – a person from the Philippines who is living and working in another country – is not easy. Most people think it is a promise of a good life. Yes, I get to earn more than what I could earn in my country, and I'm able to provide a better future for my family. On the other hand, not everyone is aware of the hard work and sacrifices I need to make to be able to give my family a comfortable life. But it's always a great feeling when I receive my salary; that means I'm able to send money again to my loved ones for their daily expenses, particularly during the time when my younger sister was studying in college.

I thank God so much because He is always there for me, giving me comfort and strength. I pray hard for Him to always help me overcome all of my struggles, and I make sure I have constant communication with my family. I'm also grateful for all of my friends, who also support me.

Living and working abroad for almost 28 years has been an adventure – often challenging – and an experience that will remain with me for life. There's always the feeling of homesickness and loneliness, worries about my family and not being able to enjoy the traditional holidays and celebrations. But I'm so thankful that I have been given this opportunity to travel to different countries and to work at the same time. This has been an incredible learning experience. Each person I meet and any trials or pains offer new perspectives and new opportunities for growth.

I've also learned from my never-ending journey of life to seek God first. I know that He will guide me and direct my path to find true fulfillment.

A Personal Glimpse of Maidee

Maidee A. Mabale is proud to be single. She enjoys having the full freedom to make decisions about everything in her life. She resides in Istanbul, Turkey and works for PayPorter as a cashier. She wishes to visit some countries she admires like the United States, Canada, Paris and London.

Maidee believes that life is beautiful because it is constantly changing and evolving. She realizes that the road to success is always under construction and always moving forward, and she feels you can truly get the most out of your life.

Maria Greaves

My separation with my husband has been the hardest struggle I've been through in my life. Of course, I felt alone, and I pitied myself at first, but I said to myself, "*Cancel, cancel, cancel!*" I didn't want to go back to depression again. I just focused on being a great mother to my son and kept myself busy. I also went back to work and attended a personal growth course that changed my life into a better one, for which I'm so grateful.

The most valuable lesson that I have learned from overcoming this hardship was that life must go on. I actually felt my freedom since I experienced being controlled. That's why I was so thankful to be able to do what I wanted to do. I believe I am powerful and that I don't need a man. LOL! I can live on my own. But most of all, I got back my ultimate power through courses and programs inspired by Tony Robbins.

In all of my life's struggles, I get closer to God, who is my refuge and my strength. God is always there to help me in times of trouble.

A Personal Glimpse of Maria

Maria Nieves Santos-Greaves, the clinic manager for Surrey Hearing Care, said, "I am very passionate about my calling in hearing." She has nurtured Surrey Hearing Care since 2009 with a mission to improve the lives of people with hearing loss through better hearing, at both the consumer and industrial levels. More people – young and old and of various races – can now hear better through the quality of service Maria and her staff provide. The slogan of her company, "*Helping You Hear the World*," says it all.

Through the years, Maria has made sure that the company's mobile hearing clinic van provides free hearing tests to mainstream, visible minorities and First Nations wherever the need arises. For her tireless efforts to give back to the community, she was voted across Canada as one of the "Top 25 Immigrants" in 2015. She was a 2015 and 2016 finalist for the "Surrey Women in Business Award," in the entrepreneur category. She was awarded in 2015 as one of the "100 Most Influential Filipina Women in the World." She is also a Rotary Foundation Paul Harris Fellow awardee.

With a BS degree in pharmacy from Centro Escolar University, Philippines, Maria pursued further training in hearing instrumentation at MacEwan University in Edmonton, Alberta and at the International Hearing Society. She is multilingual and can speak English, Tagalog, Cebuano and conversational Spanish. She is also a speaker and resource person in various industry seminars, conventions and symposiums.

Maria V

I Live for Him

I am self-employed, semi-retired and a single parent with four beautiful children. I have lived my life in many shapes, at different times, with all kinds of challenges, and I am so blessed that I am still here to write this short message to share with you.

Taking care of a cancer patient requires a lot of patience and love. In August 1993, after one year of serving my sick husband, who was given only one or two years to live, I became a single parent at age 42. As a self-employed mother of a three-year-old son and three other older children, I struggled. But with some funds left by my late husband, including the survivorship benefits being given to us from his pension, I was given an opportunity to purchase my new home, with the help of my parents. With a strong faith and great determination, I pushed myself to survive.

A year passed, and fortunately, the real estate business started to soar high, so I got into buying insurance policies for myself and my children, setting up my SEP-IRA, buying some stocks and investing in several properties. We lived a very comfortable life!

However, life, as they say, has ups and downs, so another big challenge in my life came during the years 2009 to 2011, when the worst recession banged the whole country and my real estate business (my main source of income) was seriously slammed! No sales and no income for those years! I depleted all of my savings, had to sell all of my stocks, took out all of my cash values from our insurance policies and then filed for bankruptcy. With several properties I had in jeopardy, including my own residence, I was left in limbo, with nowhere and no one to run to. There seemed to be no way at all!

I remember sobbing for days and days in my room, kneeling and begging the Lord for mercy. I said, "I worked so hard, was honest in all my dealings and faithful in giving my tithes. I donated to and helped many who were in need, and I tried by every means to keep a good, if not excellent, credit standing. I did not miss church." I poured out my heavy heart, asking why and when this lack would end. With my almost-fading faith and exhausted efforts to get back on track, I stopped questioning and cried heavily to the Lord, surrendering all of my debts, lack, frustrations, fears, doubts, anger and helplessness to Him. God whispered back, "Be still and know that I am God" (Ps. 46:10), and "Many are the plans in a person's heart, but it is the Lord's purpose that prevails." (Prov. 19:21).

Days went by, and with a new purpose in life, I strove to find work and tried so hard to negotiate with the banks and creditors, hoping to settle things. They did not listen! I had to account for every penny I was receiving and allot it to best use it for our survival. Everything seemed to be so tight, but the blessing is that our family bonding became tighter than I had ever imagined it would be.

Today, I have to thank my past for where and who I am right now. I was taught what God's purpose was for me. The Lord had some ways of rebuilding my relationship with Him. I knew in my heart that He would never forsake me; He already has a plan for me, and it is the best plan. I just have to believe, put Him first, follow His plan and do everything for His glory. And everything else will follow.

Believe me then as I relate this to you now: God saved ALL of my properties! How? Just believe. He did! It is another great testimony to share, so briefly, I was able to sell my building two years ago and one piece of land in California and I still have my other properties in California and a nice investment condo. The best thing is, I am still living in the same house with the same real estate business and having more projects God is blessing me with day by day. And all of my children have good jobs that we can all be proud of.

We have added to the family a kind-hearted son-in-law (who always claims to be my favorite!), a lovely daughter-in-law who married my medical doctor son, and five beautiful grandchildren whom I get to visit this holiday season. We are truly blessed and will always keep in our hearts God's words: "Do not be afraid; do not be discouraged, for the Lord your God will be with you wherever you go." (Josh. 1:9 NIV).

Yes! We know now our true purpose in life: We live for Him. And I pray that you and your family live for Him, too!

A Personal Glimpse of Maria

Maria V is the third in a family of nine children. Her late father was a reputable orthopedic surgeon. Her retired mother was a nutrition teacher. She graduated high school from a private girls' school and college from the University of the Philippines with a BS degree in education, with a major in biology.

Right after college, she trained for three months to be a speech pathologist in a hospital, and then worked in a US-based insurance company for almost a year. Maria became a marketing assistant in a prestigious real estate development company, and eventually she was the advertising and marketing director of a big commercial center for almost seven years, where she developed good relationships with owners and managers of big establishments and department stores. Later, she built and ran a restaurant of their own, then moved to work for pension plan programs and became a licensed insurance agent and won several awards in sales.

Maria moved to the United States, where she and her late husband put up a fish factory and a food distribution company in California. After that, they moved to Washington State, where she became a licensed real estate broker and a licensed insurance producer, which she still is.

As a lover of music and the arts, Maria has been involved for a number of years in producing and promoting musical and cultural shows and various fundraising projects in the community. She also serves in a church council in one of the Christian churches in the Pacific Northwest.

Nancy Martinez

One of the biggest struggles that I have gone through was caring for my mother and raising my four children as a single mother. I worked graveyard shifts to support my family. After getting home from work and getting the kids ready, I found time to sleep in my car after dropping them off to elementary school in the morning and to preschool in the early afternoon. I set my alarm for when it was time to pick them up. We would then head home, where I would make dinner and help them with homework. After putting the kids to sleep, I would finally be able to catch a couple more hours of sleep before going to work from 11 p.m. to 7 a.m. I did this for eight years straight, until all of my children made it into high school. The same routine, every day of the week – I tirelessly did it out of love for my children.

I overcame this struggle by staying positive and by focusing on my *"why."* My children were my reason why I never gave up! On days where I was too physically and mentally drained, my mom was always there to help me take care of the children. I can't truly say that I was perfect in every way, because no one is perfect. What I can say is that I truly did my absolute best, and I am so very proud of that!

A definite lesson that I learned from going through this time of my life is "*grit*," which is having the courage to stand up and fight for what you believe in. I could have given up and stopped fighting on countless occasions, but I chose not to. When times are rough, I always look into the future and ask myself what life would be like for my children if I quit now. I couldn't give up on them.

Seeing today how my children have grown into loving, happy and ambitious adults shows me that I put in all those graveyard shifts for a reason. As they move forward in life with families of their own, I can't help but feel like the luckiest grandma in the world.

A Personal Glimpse of Nancy

Nancy Martinez was born in San Diego, San Pablo City, Laguna, Philippines on October 29, 1960. She is the youngest of eight siblings. Her parents were Josefa Ilaw and Reynaldo Martinez. She attended elementary and secondary school at Laguna College. However, she moved to Canada in the middle of her fourth year of high school on November 14, 1977 and lived with her family in North Vancouver. She stayed there for a few years until she got married in 1981 to her late ex-husband, Carlos Perez. During the first several years of their marriage, they moved a few times around North Vancouver, until they finally decided to move to Vancouver in 1987. They had four children – Veronica, Eugene, Maria and Jeremy. After selling the home she co-owned with her brother, Nancy used the profits from the sale to purchase her family's very first home in Vancouver, and the rest was history!

Nancy loves dancing, travelling and having fun with colleagues and friends.

Ning Mah

At age 38, I was diagnosed with stage II metastatic breast cancer and decided to have a bilateral mastectomy. I had both of my breasts removed and had breast reconstruction. After I had 16 shots of chemotherapy and 30 days of radiation; I believed that with a positive attitude, I would be able to kick my cancer to the curb with little problem. Knowing that I have my husband, family, friends and especially my two children, I couldn't just give in to this monster disease. I realized I still wanted to do so much with my children; I wanted to see them grow up and have families of their own and to see how their futures would turn out.

So I was on a mission to fight this disease, and I would not let it get to me. I also knew that with medical science and research, I could beat this so-called cancer. I never thought of it as a bad situation or that I was the unlucky one. I looked at it as if I had a cold that was just stopping by and eventually would go away. I didn't let it run my life but instead I looked ahead into the future. I am young; I have so much to give, so much to accomplish. I want to explore the world, so I said to myself, "I am in control of my life, and nobody or nothing – not even cancer – will take that away from me." I want to live!

I learned: that a positive attitude is the key to overcoming any misfortune that you may have in your life; to always look forward and not backward; that there are others out there who have no access to medical help or resources like I do; and that I am the lucky one because I have been given that chance to fight: All I have to do is show up.

A Personal Glimpse of Ning

Ning Santiago Mah was born in Manila, Philippines. She moved to Vancouver at age 16. She has worked for a currency exchange company for many years, dealing with currency trades. She has two children and has spent most of her life dedicating her free time to supporting their sports activities. She loves to spend her summer months camping across British Columbia with her family. She loves the ocean, travelling to islands and exploring the unknown across the globe.

When things get tougher, Ning always recalls this beautiful quote from the Dalai Lama: "Choose to be optimistic – it feels better."

Nori Lumbera-Villaruel

As far back as I can remember, I have been through a number of struggles in almost all stages of my life. Being born poor, marked with a challenging childhood, and as the eldest in the family, it was heartbreaking to feel the needs that we couldn't have fulfilled: beautiful clothes, shoes, toys, etc., and most of the time, we were discriminated against. My parents were not earning enough for basic needs, and it was sad seeing other children enjoying their lives to the fullest, while we only watched them silently.

I still recall my father once saying, "My ultimate dream is to see my children graduate high school." Luckily, we were able to reach college. I finished at De La Salle Araneta, Metro Manila with a BS degree in agriculture. I had a few jobs, even working in United Arab Emirates.

There came a point in my career when I needed to make a decision: I gave up my position and was transferred to the local government, where I had accepted a lower position just to get in. From there, my promotions came very quickly. Now I have a stable job and good income as a department head in the local government. I am fortunate to be able to use my position to extend services to the community.

I live a comfortable life with my family, though we are not rich. Challenges are always there. I lost my youngest brother four years ago, following a heart attack. There is nothing so painful as a sudden loss. Last year, my husband died, due to cardiac arrest, and just recently, my father died of old age. I felt that I lost a significant portion of happiness, but I have to stand strong with these natural courses of life.

With all of the challenges I have faced in life, I have been able to overcome them by using my greatest weapons, which are courage, humility and faith in God. The Bible says "he who exalts himself will be humbled, and he who humbles himself will be exalted by God" (Matt 23:12 NIV). Added to that, I have worked hard and have done the best I can in everything I do, in order to prove that I am more of an asset than a liability. It is always my principle not to disappoint those who have placed their trust in me.

I am not after riches as I always remember that whatever wealth we have, at the end of the day, we all will be leaving empty-handed. I am happy with what I already have, and I thank God, knowing that there are so many people around the globe who do not have any of what I have. For me, success is not about having material possessions; what is truly important is finding fulfillment in whatever we do and sharing our blessings with others.

A Personal Glimpse of Nori

Nori Lumbera-Villaruel was born on February 13, 1963 at Dolores, Province of Quezon to Norberto Lumbera and Heda Romero. She was the eldest, followed by a brother who is a businessman, then another brother who is an official of the Philippine National Police, her entrepreneur sister and her youngest brother, who is deceased.

From 1976 to 1980, Nori attended high school at San Pablo Colleges, where Marissa Magcawas was the class valedictorian and her close friend. She continued her college education at De La Salle Araneta in Metro Manila, where she finished her BS degree in agriculture. Her professional civil service eligibility qualified her for employment in the government. She also took and passed the licensure examination for environmental planners. She is the treasurer of the Quezon Local Planners Association and a member of the League of Local Planning and Development Coordinators of the Philippines, Inc. and the Philippine Institute of Environmental Planners.

She is currently the head of the municipal planning and development department in Dolores, Quezon, with a number of affiliations on almost all committees and special bodies of the local government. She is Nori Lumbera-Villaruel, happily serving for the development of our community.

Norman Carriere

Having been born in a small town out in the country, I always felt special as a child, always inquiring about life and its special meanings. My mother, whom I always thought was normal, was diagnosed with bipolar disorder right after the birth of her first child. Six months after the diagnosis, my grandma, who to this day is one of the strongest person I've ever met, showed up at the hospital with a picture of my oldest sister's hand – and footprints drawn on a piece of paper and proceeded to tell my mom, "Your daughter needs you at home!" This action snapped my mom back to reality, and she became a mother for the first time.

Fast-forward to some 40 years later: Some friends introduced me to a personal growth program, where I learned a lot about myself in overcoming incomprehensible challenges. You see, as I grew up, my mom had multiple relapses with her mental illness. To my understanding now, every seven years, she would re-attempt suicide. The first time I was too young to remember; my aunt told me I might have been four years old, crying and asking why the ambulance man was taking away my mom. Some serious and unconscious depression appeared at that age, and eventually I asked myself, why me?

The relevance to the personal growth program is that it helped me to overcome stress and to understand that as we grow up, our existence is made up of a series of events; the stronger the event, the harder it marks you, just like a blueprint in your deep subconscious. For me, when things would get good, they would then fall apart, approximately every seven years; two examples of this are the breakdown of both my marriage and my relationship with my daughter. In this personal growth course, through a series of mind meditation exercises, I was able to review some of the hardships I'd experienced as a child after multiple attempts; prior to that, I only drew blanks. This dictated a lot of the directions I chose in my life and where I would eventually end up! For me, it was sales, sales, sales – until my marriage broke down and I was burnt out! Then I made a big change: I went into the healing arts. Yes, I wanted to heal myself by helping others heal themselves.

Our mind is very powerful; if things are not quite right, confide in someone you know and trust. This story goes out to you, the reader, as you may very well be the person who could end up saving someone's life. When we listen, compassion comes through, and then there is hope for all of us to be heard and to start healing at the very roots of our souls. God will never give you a problem you cannot handle. Try it: Go ahead and trust your intuition, and you will find out that God is an intricate part of your gut feeling.

Through personal growth courses, prayers and trusting and evaluating my own self-worth, I was able to overcome challenges in my life. Discovering my purpose in life and getting to know and accept who I really am were some of the most valuable lessons I have learned through this journey.

A Personal Glimpse of Norman

Norman Carriere is a father of two well-educated, young-adult daughters. He has always been a hard worker with a heart of gold. Norman worked in the telecommunications industry for most of his career. He then gravitated toward the healing arts, helping individuals learn more about healing themselves through better health, proper hydration, understanding good nutrition and stress management. While Norman's infectious smile has attracted amazing friendships, throughout his career, he has been able to cement great work relationships while building successful hearing clinics for the last 13 years. He is also a keen believer in Napoleon Hill's book *Think and Grow Rich*. What are you thinking right now?

Perla Martinez

The hardest struggle I have had was when our family was separated because of immigration problems in the United States. My husband and children were ordered to leave the country because of our illegal status; we had overstayed our time in the United States. I was allowed to stay, as my mother, an American citizen, was petitioning for me. I went into depression because I couldn't bear to be separated from my family, which was always my priority, so I couldn't endure being away from them.

At this point in my life, when I hit rock bottom, I realized that I needed to hold on to God. I had to let go and let God. In my prayers, I told God that it was no longer *my* will be done, but *His*. Then, I was advised by a friend that they were accepting professionals in Canada, so I applied, with my family as my dependents, and I was approved within a short period of time.

After waiting one year from application to approval, we landed in Canada. I knew in my heart that God was with us through this journey. To summarize, I lifted everything to God and let Him control my life. I found the peace here in Canada that was elusive to us in the United States.

My valuable lesson is, "We are nothing without the Lord." We can never be truly happy unless our lives are in accordance with God's will.

A Personal Glimpse of Perla

Perla Martinez has been happily married to Joseph Martinez for 49 years. They have three children – Joyce, Iris and P.J. –who are all married, and she has five grandchildren. Perla and her family immigrated to Canada from the United States and have been happily living here for the last 20 years. Perla and Joseph are members of "Couples for Christ" and "Foundation for Family and Life," which is the community that the Lord used to draw them to Him intimately. They have been serving in the community for the past 18 years and will continue to do so for as long as they can.

Perla is blissfully retired and enjoys travelling the world. For her, travelling creates memories, and she gains new friends, new experiences and new stories in her lifetime. She believes that it also improves her overall health. Oftentimes, she travels while serving the community in renewing and strengthening Christian values and sharing the gospel.

Remilia Lopez Chiong

One of the hardest struggles in my life was living with a drug-dependent husband who risked our life with our kids. Our daily existence was very difficult, as we tried to survive and thrive with no peace of mind. In addition, we faced death, terrifying ordeals and tough and trying times.

On August 22, 1982, a tragedy and traumatic experience occurred when there was a massacre in Bongao, Tawi-Tawi, in our own residence, where our father's second cousin sprayed 90 bullets due to land disputes. Our beloved father was killed; my mother was in Laguna. On September 17, 2007, another tragic event happened when our rented apartment was razed by fire in Sta. Maria, Zamboanga City. All of our things were burned into ashes except the clothes we were wearing at the time.

These traumatic events caused me strong feelings of fear, sadness and grief. I felt hopeless, too, but I realized that prayer was the best weapon to overcome all kinds of struggles in my life. Moreover, by holding on to my hope, trust and faith in our sovereign, Almighty God through our Lord Jesus Christ, with the saving and healing power of the Holy Spirit, through fervent and earnest prayers; I believe that God will see us through to overcome all of the challenges of life.

I've learned in my life's journey to face life squarely, to courageously move on in a positive and right attitude, and to live life to the fullest. Likewise, I believe that in everything that happens in my life, God is still in control, and that God can create beauty out of the shattered pieces of my life. If gold can be tested through fire, the human character must be tested through the furnace of humiliation when we humble ourselves before Almighty God. For God knows the plans are for us to prosper – not to be harmed – and plans that give us a future and hope. Apart from God, we are nothing, and we can do nothing. Nothing is impossible and hard unto our God. He will fight the battles for us. Romans 8:31 asks, "When God is for us, who can be against us?" The "weapons of our warfare are not carnal but mighty through God in the pulling down of strongholds" (2 Cor. 10:4) in our lives.

My goal is to live a purpose-driven life in accordance with the highest and most perfect will of God. If I put God first in everything I do, He will crown all my efforts with success and prosperity, for He holds my future.

A Personal Glimpse of Remilia

Remilia Lopez Chiong is a proud mother of six amazing children. She graduated with a BA degree in public administration in 1986. She then took some units for her master's in business administration the following year. While raising her children, Remilia continued studying, taking a certificate of government management in 2003 from Mindanao State University. Her passion for studying continued and she attained a master's degree in public administration in April 2006 from the same university.

Remilia loves to attend seminars, workshops, trainings, conferences and conventions, as she believes that they offer numerous benefits, including improving communication skills, gaining expert knowledge, networking with others and renewing motivation and confidence.

She is responsible, highly organized, dynamic, innovative, resourceful and articulate in communication, and her managerial and entrepreneurial skills help her to perform her job in a very efficient and effective manner.

Lingkat, as she's fondly called by many, loves to travel and visit her children and grandkids. She is a big supporter of totally eliminating the garbage on the streets through proper waste disposal and management. She mentions that we should be paying attention in disposing our trash and always look for opportunities to recycle or compost it for the betterment of our environment and the world we live in.

Rohan Baichu

As the country of Guyana was going through a political and economic turmoil, I migrated to Canada, where I aspired to become a professional boxer. There, I would face numerous challenges, but the biggest of all was being an immigrant without legal work status, which meant it was a battle to earn a living. This would continue for the three years I spent in Canada before moving to the United States with hopes of accomplishing my dreams, which by then included furthering my education.

Arriving in New York City, and being without legal status, I managed to find work but at the bare minimum wage. The process of working low-end jobs and training on a thin budget led to sporadic injuries, which, after another five years, led me to abandoning my boxing goals and pursuing a more traditional path in life. Needless to say, I stumbled at times, but I kept on trying to improve my station in life. At the age of 29 – 10 years after I had left Guyana – I finally gained legal status.

Amidst all of the economic and social hardships, two main factors helped me to maintain a positive attitude. First and foremost was the ability to stay focused and maintain a high energy level, no matter what the situation was. This was done by prioritizing on an almost daily basis; I had a workout program that consisted of mainly running and calisthenics, in local parks or less-trafficked streets, since a gym membership was not economically feasible. Throughout my life, I have sworn to the magical effects of a great workout as a stress-buster, no matter what problems I'm faced with. Although I'm not very religious, I also believe in meditative silence, which can be practiced even on a moving train, as a means of gaining clarity of mind amidst a sea of confusion. With this approach, I find myself dealing with frustrations, disappointments and overall hardships in a calm and more strategic manner, as my ability to exercise patience increases when required.

Even though I never achieved my goal of being a world champion boxer, I was able to represent my country as a track athlete and also completed three years of college, along with some technical and vocational courses. Twenty years after leaving Guyana, and adhering to the principle of a "daily grind," I achieved a significant level of success when one of the top teams in the world of professional sports, the New York Yankees, offered me a highly coveted slot on their training staff. With this climb up the ladder of my life from the bottom rung, my situation and that of my family was significantly transformed from that of a low-income wage earner to a more stable position in just about every aspect. This advancement enabled my family and me to gain a bit of self-esteem and accompanying validation for what had seemed — and, at least in my mind, had felt — like a lifetime of failure to that point.

Obviously, the years of perseverance, while not leading to my earlier goals, had produced a high measure of success. I had learned, albeit painstakingly slowly, that the road to success detours into avenues and alleyways that sometimes dead-end into a destination of failure. That failure taught me how to re-evaluate and chart a new course and that overcoming obstacles is just part of the process of life. My ability to remain calm and focused was severely challenged at times, especially when goals and expectations defied the realities of my situation. Mistakes were made along the way, as errors in judgment occurred, but my adherence to the principle of attending to even one minor task on a daily basis was probably the most valuable tool I had in my 20-year quest for a better life.

A Personal Glimpse of Rohan

Rohan Baichu was born in then-British Guian (now independent Guyana), on March 15, 1959, into a family of 12 children. His mother and father were subsistence farmers and in the rural part of a colonial, Third World country, that meant life on a farm from sunrise to sunset. After graduating high school at the age of 17, Rohan became a schoolteacher on a fast-track teaching program, and then he joined the Guyana Army and later migrated to Canada.

Rohan believes that a great workout and meditative silence, which he enjoys the most, continuously help him to maintain a positive attitude. He also recognizes that it is maintaining a healthy lifestyle that has enabled him to make better decisions, as the mind and body function best as a unit of one. Meditative silence helped him to realize the value of prayer, to form a connection with the Supreme Being and to maintain that connection consciously in every action he takes. The value of patience was a hard lesson for an ambitious, clueless young man to learn, Rohan discovered.

In summary, Rohan realized that his life was a microcosm of the world in which he lived: a world where there is good and bad and everything else in between. He feels that his belief in himself and the fact that he is a force for good – no how tiny the amount – has led him to have a positive self-image, thus enabling him to not succumb to the pressure of high expectations but still keep the goal in mind.

THE POWER OF 26

Vernon Magcawas

During my time at Metro Drug, Inc., I didn't have any problems with my payables because the management is mandated by law to make such deductions as SSS, PhilHealth contributions, and most especially the Pag-IBIG Fund, in which I had a large number of deductions, due to a house and lot purchase loan. The problem occurred when I left the company. I was obliged to pay my Pag-IBIG loan each month. As time passed by, the loan was overlooked, unattended and unpaid, which resulted in an increasing interest rate, tripling the amount I owed, so I could not pay the whole amount. I was given a deadline; I made a compromised decision that I had to pay a huge amount within three months. It was really worrisome and alarming because confiscation of property would be implemented if I did not comply.

How important was the house and lot – my property? A place to eat, sleep, feel safe, laugh and even cry, a place to live in was really important to my family. The place we called "*home*" helped to strengthen our relationship and bound us in unity and love. Never-ending memories resided in my house. I couldn't afford to lose that property.

Undoubtedly, I looked for solutions to this problem, such as generating resources just to pay the loan and then save the property. I decided to sell products to different trade outlets to make more profits, maximizing my time through regular visits to them, and increasing the frequency of calls to potential customers, so familiarity would help me to make more sales.

Thank God, I'm very lucky and was able to completely pay the entire amount of the loan. Now we are very happy and thankful that we have the certified copy of the property title.

It is indeed true that any problems in life have solutions. I never give up; by setting my mind freely and confidently focusing on constructive ideas, I can overcome any barrier that obstructs access to my goals. I learned to pray to God all the time, because He always provides, protects and guides by all means, up to the last minute of my life. I am also thankful and appreciative because God is always my partner to shoulder all the burdens that I've encountered in everyday living. To lean on God, cast my cares on Him and trust Him at all times are notable words that I abide by.

A Personal Glimpse of Vernon

Vernon L. Magcawas is married to Remedios Ferrera Magcawas. He is 60 years old, with three lovely daughters: Anne Charmaigne, Lara Isabela, and Christelle Arianne, who have all graduated in their chosen fields. Presently, he is managing a small convenience store and delivering different generic and branded medicines and other medical supplies to various drug outlets. This produces a more sustainable income for the family's daily living and expenses.

Vernon enjoys traveling to different places with his family. They also love to go on picnics and outings, which they consider a fun and healthy way to spend quality time with each other. While enjoying his life, he always reminds himself and his family to *"never give up"* when challenges come, but to believe in themselves, and to simply find ways to make things work – and they will, in God's perfect timing.

Yolanda Tanciangco

Life is full of challenges and trials, but the hardest struggle that I have been through so far was when I got sick while raising my three wonderful boys. It was very tough because of the financial obligations and the difficulties maintaining family functions and a sense of routine, as I was always the one responsible for that. Due to the lack of time with my children, I was concerned about the negative impact this might have on them. But with the love of my family and friends, and their outpouring of support, my family and I were able to pass through this storm.

I'm fortunate to be surrounded by many positive people, and because I have an upbeat attitude, the pains and struggles did not make me quit or give up; instead, I kept moving forward. Having an optimistic outlook is the most valuable thing. I always implement it when faced with challenges. It helps me to cope more easily with my daily affairs, brings optimism into my life and makes it easier to avoid worries and negative thinking.

Just like the trials in our lives, typhoons or storms appear as well, and we don't know when they will hit us, how strong they will be, or where they will occur. They come and go; it's the same with our challenges. The question is, how do we deal with the aftermath of the storms in our lives? Remember the saying,

"The greater your storm, the brighter your rainbow." Let's learn to embrace our storms; the sun always shines its brightest after the biggest ones.

A Personal Glimpse of Yolanda

Yolanda Tanciangco is proud mother of three wonderful sons and a loving wife to an amazing man. She was born in Pampanga, Philippines. She owns an employment agency and loves to help people find work, particularly the live-in caregivers who come from different countries. Since December 1996, she has been helping many people to come to Canada and get employment. She is also the owner/wholesale distributor of Coffee King Plus, a premixed, all-in-one instant coffee with spirulina ganoderma extract. Yolanda has lots of happy clients drinking her coffee product.

Yolanda is very good at sales and has performed excellently in multi-level marketing. She enjoys volunteering, even though she has a busy life and hardly finds time to give back. She is also passionate about feeding less-fortunate kids. She has a feeding program in her hometown, and this is one of her missions when celebrating her birthday.

A SPECIAL MESSAGE FROM
TYRELL J. MAGCAWAS

My name is **Tyrell Magcawas;** I am the only son of Marissa Magcawas. In my 20 years of living, I've made plenty of mistakes: some small ones and even some big ones. I believe that if you're not making mistakes in life, you're doing something wrong. Mistakes are opportunities to learn, to become a better person and to move on. I think the greatest lessons are actually learned at the worst times from the worst mistakes, because they make us mentally stronger.

For myself, my biggest mistake was not believing in myself the way others believed in me. The crazy thing is that I have such a big support group that is always telling me these great things about myself. But what was missing was my self-confidence and self-assurance. I've always had a mindset of just doing the minimum, since I was accustomed to failure. However, I learned that failure is a part of life, and all that matters is the bounce-back.

It started with learning about and taking a closer look at some important things about myself. I kept reminding myself that I'm bound to get better and to not beat myself up. I have also learned that, at the end of the day, I have to put myself first before anyone else because that's the only thing I've got. Once I realized how to be at peace with myself and my life, everything around me feels so much more relaxed, and the world glows differently.

My Mother Is a Warrior

Whatever challenges, trials and pains that come my mom's way, she overcomes them and always comes out a winner. Even in the most frustrating situation, she finds the good and positive side of it. She turns worries into opportunities and uses failures as stepping-stones. She is bold, courageous and always taking risks. She manages to embrace the tribulations, no matter how difficult they are, and that's why my mother is a warrior!

March 28, 2014 was an unforgettable day: My mother was diagnosed with breast cancer. Just thinking about that day brings tears to my eyes. I literally thought my life was over; it was like getting hit by something and taking your last breath. I'm sure you can relate or feel the pain of someone so close to you going through something that is almost incurable. I felt as though things weren't the same, and just seeing my mom going through all the pains, I asked God for one more chance: a chance to make things right, to be more appreciative, to spend time with her whenever she asked, to say "*thank you*" more often, to say "*I love you*" and to tell her, "*It's going to be okay*" when thing got rough. All my life, I just wanted to make her proud because I am her only child, and to me, she is the greatest mother anyone could ask for.

Over the last few years, it's been hard on her mentally and physically, but I have watched her rise into a stronger woman; a year later, she was cancer-free! I can't explain how proud I am of her! She's one of the strongest women I know, and the most caring and loving. I couldn't ask for a more supportive mom. She, also being a single parent and going through that all alone just amazes me; it demonstrates the kind of person I want to be. I can't thank her enough for everything she's done and for always pushing me to go beyond my limits to be the young man I am today.

The moral behind this experience is to never mistreat the people who care about you, who appreciate you and love you the most and to give them the same love and respect that they give you, because you never know when it could be the last time you ever see them or say, "I love you." I know I have grown into a better person after this experience, and I've learned to always be grateful and respectful and to always say, "I love you," because we never know if we will get another moment. Tomorrow is never promised.

ABOUT THE AUTHOR

On January 11, 1964, a precious child was born to proud parents Osias and Ernita Magcawas, and that was *me*, a happy, playful, beautiful girl named Marissa Magcawas. I am the sixth child of eight siblings. I was born in San Diego, San Pablo City, Philippines.

I'm so thankful for my childhood and family. Although we grew up poor, our parents instilled the importance of education into our minds. They made sure that all of us finished our chosen careers. I graduated from Philippine Women's University with a BA degree in communication arts. I was grateful that I had the privilege of going to any university of my choice, to take any course I wanted to. I had a full scholarship for one year of my education, as I had graduated valedictorian at San Pablo Colleges.

Going to university was the first chance for me to live independently; as it was the first time I had moved away from my parents and family. It was tough to manage things on my own and to adjust to city life in Manila, but it was worth it. It was exciting as I begin to figure out who I was and who and what I wanted to be. I gained wonderful friends. I became a staff writer in our school newspaper. Unfortunately, I did not maintain my academic scholarship. However, I got accepted into another form of scholarship, wherein I got to work at the registrar's office. University was the time when I realized my independence and learned important lessons.

ABOUT THE AUTHOR

On January 1991, I landed in beautiful British Columbia, Canada, which I now call home. I came here as a live-in caregiver or nanny. After coming here from the Philippines and working as an executive assistant in the advertising department of a prestigious company, and then suddenly being confined to just the four corners of the house, doing household chores and taking care of kids – call me crazy, but it was not an easy transition. It was a shock at first; I just had to accept my present reality, something that I have almost perfected over the years. Once I accepted my reality and was not in denial anymore, things become easier. I'm thankful for working as a nanny because the experience helped me to hone my patience, maturity, understanding, sound judgment, nurturing spirit and genuine love for children. I was actually hired by a college as an accounting administrator, due to my being a nanny. The principal was so impressed with the kind of flexibility and well-rounded personality that I possess. So, kudos to all of the live-in nannies and caregivers; continue the great job you're doing!

March 28, 2023, marked the nine-year anniversary of my breast cancer diagnosis. This breast cancer journey is one of the most painful moments in my life, especially with the side effects of chemotherapy, the mastectomy procedure and the healing process. Nonetheless, I consider this was the best time because I felt so close to God. I fully surrendered myself to Him; I received Jesus Christ as my personal savior.

I was at the calmest point in my life, at the most peaceful place within myself and with all the people around me. I healed very well while continuing with my work in progress with the Lord. This journey had been difficult, but the prayers and loving support, combined with each word of kindness, had seen me through and made this battle worth all the treasure in the world. Breast cancer changed me in so many ways: It got me closer to God who created me; I learned the value of meaningful relationships, and truly appreciated life in significantly simple ways.

My breast cancer journey has also, in a strange way, done some amazing things for me. It has allowed me to be more *me*; I'm much more in touch with who I am – my beingness, my true self and my higher purpose in life. I took some steps backwards and got a closer and better view of my life. I started to slow down and relax, saying *"No"* when I deemed it necessary and it felt good. Most importantly, I realized how strong I am as a person with God's continued guidance and unconditional love.

Yes, some things have changed, and this battle has changed my life. But the change can be beautiful, and lovely things can happen in trying times, too. And this book, *Stumbling: Life's Great Lessons in Overcoming Challenges, Trials and Pains*, is one of the best outcomes.

I was having a great ride in my life, right after my breast cancer, when a mishap occurred; I had a car accident in 2015. Thank God, I was alive! However, I was diagnosed with depression and post-traumatic stress disorder. I decided then to seek professional help and to take every step necessary to cure myself. I realized that if there is a physical sickness, there is mental illness; my brain is a part of my body that needs care and treatment. My simple analogy made things easier for me. I can attest that my depression and anxiety are real, and only someone who has been through it, or a psychologist and psychiatrist, would comprehend. Let it be known that mental health disorders have severe consequences and need to be taken seriously.

This challenge has been difficult, and it has affected my son in crucial ways, oftentimes negatively, especially because he's a growing teenager. I felt bad, sad and guilty because of the way I treated him sometimes. On the bright side, this ongoing journey is perfecting my patience, enhancing my resilience and making me closer to God.

I became fully aware that there's no quick fix to life's discomfort, specifically my battle with PTSD and depression. I concluded it is okay not to be okay sometimes. It's okay to seek support and help and share inner struggles to someone willing to listen; it does get better every day. As I go through life, with all of its adversities and challenges, I continue to practice changing the way I look at the world and always see the good side of things and people. My intentions are genuine and positive. Then my life is transformed, putting me into a better position.

Over the years, I have learned to be spontaneous, to be bold and courageous, to practice being in the now, to live one day at a time, to simplify life and to seize and enjoy the moment. As Rick Pitino says, "Learning to live in the present tense – one that's free from the failures of the past and the anxieties of the future – is a wonderful gift and one you always should be striving for."

Moreover, it is with my great pride and honor that I continuously involve myself in various non-profit organizations, community projects and events that inspire future generations and are committed to help support those who are in need. I know that I am making a difference in my own little ways, and that there is no greater pleasure than making a contribution to community projects with meaning, purpose and passion.

I'm grateful for all of my experiences, good or bad; for all of the struggles I've been through and overcome; for the beautiful memories; for the amazing people I have met; for the beautiful places I've been to; for my wonderful friends and my loving family. Because without them, I would not be the kind of person I have become. I may not have all the riches in the world, but with God in my life and all the marvelous people and the great support system I have, I am indeed blessed. Thank you, Lord! I'm so proud to say, *"It's great to be me!"*

I stumble, I break, I fail, I rise, I heal – I overcome. I fall, I get up, I cry, I laugh at myself and I keep moving forward. I'm a courageous single mom. I am a survivor, and I am an author.

www.ingramcontent.com/pod-product-compliance
Lightning Source LLC
Chambersburg PA
CBHW070510090426
42735CB00012B/2717